MY STORY

Lola Taubman

Compiled and edited by
Diane Kirkpatrick

Dedication

I would like to dedicate my life's story to my parents, Miksa and Zsenka, my Apuka and Anyuka, and to my brothers, Tibor, Artur, and Arnold (Nanci).

Editor's Preface

Lola Taubman has a rich, poignant, warm, and powerful story, and she tells it well. Born Ilona (Lola) Goldstein, she was swept from a lively childhood in modest-sized communities in the Carpathian Mountains of Czechoslovakia into the Holocaust. One of Lola's brothers died during the years leading to the war. Her parents and three remaining brothers all perished in the camps, as did many other relatives. Yet she and some relatives managed to escape extermination, and these banded together to help each other through the deep anguish of the death camps, and in the struggle to build new lives within the extremes of the turmoil at the end of the war and during the immediate post-war period.

After four years of persistent re-applications from DP camps in Germany, Lola found a way to secure papers that allowed her to come to the United States, where she joined relatives who had managed to come earlier. She began a new life in New York, then moved to Detroit, where she met and married Sam Taubman. At first she talked little of the dark years, and also little about the happier period of her pre-war childhood. As years passed, Lola increasingly felt it was important to speak her story, to become a witness for the history that many were saying had never happened. She began speaking for the Holocaust Education Center of Central Florida: to community groups, in schools, and to other interested groups, so that her listeners might become a collective memory of the traumatic story she had lived.

Lola is a riveting storyteller, but relatively few of her public talks were recorded. The sound-recorded interviews provided a rich data cache for creating a full text narrative that is not the usual printed essay, but rather an attempt to share the rich orality of Lola's spoken version of "My Story." This is her gift to her family, but she hopes others might wish to learn about her life's journey. Lola and her daughter Ruth asked me to help edit the mass of paper and recorded material into a book. I conducted five new interviews with Lola, which clarified and expanded important details.

My aim has been for this book's pages to capture in print the power and charm of Lola Taubman's oral telling, inevitably without the persuasive cadence of Lola's deep-throated voice, which carries overlays of her many spoken languages. The method resembles a mosaic constructed from Lola's spoken words in the variant tellings preserved in the printed and recorded files of her talks and interviews, with some light editing for the sake of coherence. I have added explanatory notes to illuminate details that might be unfamiliar to those who have not lived the history that has intersected with Lola Taubman's life. To this task I bring my undergraduate training as historian, and my long experience as art historian and editor.

List of Sources

A. Transcripts from interviews:

Video recordings of Lola Taubman's talks:

1. Florida Classroom, Lola Taubman talk in a classroom, videotaped by Karen Dahlridge, teacher, on VHS tape, dated sometime in the mid 1990's from evidence in the content. Editor's transfer from VHS into DVD movie, with transcript made from sound separated from the DVD file.

2. Glacier Hills Retirement Community, Ann Arbor, MI, June 10, 2011. Lola Taubman "My Story" public lecture. Diane Kirkpatrick videographer – editor's transcript from sound track separated from the video file.

Sound recordings of interviews with Lola Taubman:

1. Lola Taubman interviewed by Velma Grasseler, July 15, 2001, and July 2005, edited and re-shaped by Velma Grasseler and combined with some additions sent by Julie Ellis, December 8, 2009 – excerpts from editor's translation into digital file of the Velma Grasseler paper printout.

2. Lola Taubman interviewed by Julie Ellis, Ann Arbor Michigan, December 20, 2009 – editor's transcript from a copy of the sound recording.

3. Lola Taubman interviewed December 22, 2009, by Professor Sidney M. Bolkosky, William E. Stirton Professor in the Social Sciences, University of Michigan Dearborn, for the university's Voice/Vision Holocaust Survivor Oral History Archive (editor's excerpts from digital file copied from transcript on the UM-Dearborn website: http://holocaust.umd.umich.edu/)

4. Lola Taubman interviewed by Diane Kirkpatrick on February 8, 2011, February 15, 2011, March 3, 2011, March 17, 2011, and June 16, 2011, here drawn from the editor's transcripts from the digital sound recordings

B. Other Sources

1. Photocopy of hand-written letter from Magda and Louis Goldstein in Brooklyn, NY to Lola Goldstein in Frankfurt, Germany and her cousins, Manyi and Hersi, November 6, 1946 – here editor's digital translation from the copy in Lola Taubman's collection

2. Excerpts from the memoirs of Louis Goldstein, provided by his daughter Julie Ellis, and used with her permission in this book.

3. Louis and Magda Goldstein, "Szolyva and Izvor after 50 Years", printed copy of brief diary describing their trip in August 1993 back to Czechoslovakia – editor's digital translation from photocopy of text from Lola Taubman collection

4. Julie Ellis, "Return to Izvor 1993", printed copy and, generously, also a digital file. Julie Ellis plans to use this and the report by her parents on the same trip in writings about them at some time in the future, but has given gracious permission for brief excerpts to be used with credit in Lola Taubman's personal story. Here taken from the digital copy of the text.

4. Miscellaneous family photographs, scanned by the editor from Lola Taubman's collection.

5. Additional selected photographs loaned by family members from their collections.

Diane Kirkpatrick, Professor Emerita, History of Art
University of Michigan
Ann Arbor, May 2012

Table of Contents

ILLUSTRATIONS

Part I: Family and Childhood

Part II: The Troubles Begin

Part III: Holocaust and Post War Chaos

Part IV: Life in the United States

Figure 1   Map

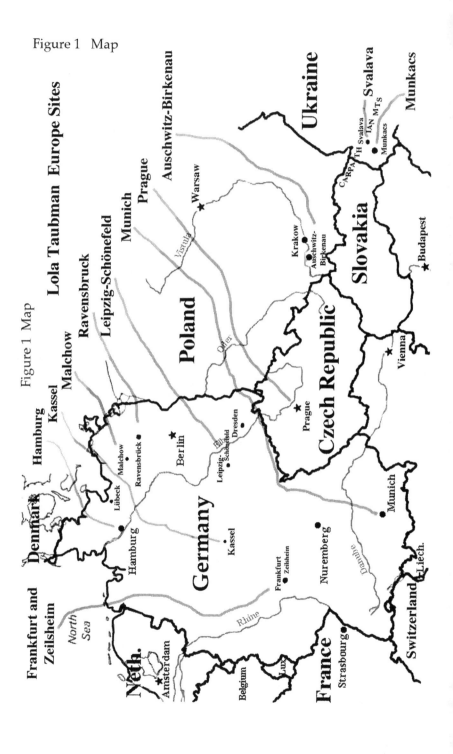

Figure 1 Map

Part I: Family and Childhood

My name is Lola Taubman. I was born in Czechoslovakia in the foothills of the Carpathian Mountains. North of us was Poland. East of us was Romania. When my parents grew up, the area was in Austria. And southeast was Hungary.[1] Then from 1918 to 1938 it became Czechoslovakia. In October 1938, as soon as the war started, Czechoslovakia was occupied by the Hungarians, but all our part of the country was cut off. At that time, our area was occupied by Ukraine. The town I come from is a small town with a name which is hard to pronounce, and its spelling changed depending on who occupied all or part of the country. Svalava is the Czechoslovakian spelling, and Szolyva is the Hungarian spelling.[2] My father's name was Max (for Maximilian) Goldstein. He was called Miksa (pronounced Miksha). My mother's name before marriage was Jenny or Zsenka Oberländer.

Family History

Zev and Esther Goldstein Family

My grandfather, William (Zev in Yiddish, with nickname Wolf) Goldstein was born in Pavlovo (or Palos) in the Carpathian Mountains on the border with Poland. My Grandmother Esther Goldstein was born in the tiny village of Izvor, which had once been called Izvor-Huta (Bireg-Forras). The villages were so close, you could walk to them. I don't know how they met. Grandmother

---

1   The region was part of the Austro-Hungarian Empire, which existed until the end of World War I, when the area containing Svalava became part of the nation of Czechoslovakia.

2   The town is now part of Ukraine, so the 2012 spelling of the town name is Svalyava.

married Grandfather at age fourteen. They lived in Izvor. At fifteen Grandmother had a child. She gave birth to fourteen children, the last was born when she was 50. Three died early, and eleven survived to adulthood. They were ten boys and one girl.

Grandfather Goldstein died in 1924 at the age of 52 of pneumonia (there was no medicine). He left my Grandmother Esther with eleven children. She had all the boys at home. The only daughter lived in the next village, so they could see each other.

Three of the older Goldstein boys—Jacob, Harry, and Ike (Isador)—came to the United States early in the century to make way for the younger ones. Ike had a nice produce business in East Brooklyn. Harry for a while was the buyer for that business in New York.

The oldest of the boys still at home in Izvor was Joseph. Then came Marcel or Martin. I called him Marci-bacsi. Bacsi means the uncle. His son, Ernö was such a smart boy. We went to the same high school, but he was older than I was. He was so good in math and literature. Next came my father, Maximilian (Miksa), who was one of twins born on October 21, 1896 (his twin died at birth). Morris came next, then Rose, then Zigmund, then David, and then Louis.

The boys grew up, one at a time, and they started to go to school. The brothers all went for eight years to the little school in Izvor. Then the boys either stayed with members of the family or with friends, and went to the school in Svalava that went up to age fourteen. The sister Rose went to the village school, too. Then she got married young and moved to a second village, which was Pavlovo (Palos).

Some sons stayed there around the vicinity in Pavlovo (Palos) and some in Izvor. Then little by little they moved into Svalava. One uncle had ten children. The others had six or seven children, and they all lost some because when the soldiers came back from the [First World] War they brought an epidemic of meningitis. Every house they lost at least one member.

Grandma's was the only Jewish family in Izvor. We loved her very much. Sometime earlier, she fell and broke her hip and never made it to the hospital, so she couldn't walk very well when we knew her. But, sitting down on a stool, she accomplished a whole lot. We took turns to come and visit Grandma. When we went, we would stay two days because the next cousins had to come—no more than two or three at a time, because we didn't sleep with Grandma.

Unfortunately, there wasn't much land to farm around Izvor, because it was in the mountains. So that wasn't very practical. Almost all the Goldsteins were in the lumber business. Uncle Joseph had a big part of a mountain, and they had the lumberjacks living right there. And they would cook, on a little fire outside, potatoes and some bacon that they had. I had a girlfriend whose father was an engineer, and they came from Poland to work for this company, and the officials had this little car, like a Jeep that ran on the railroad. We would go up there and see the lumberjacks, how they lived. And we used to go and pick raspberries in the mountain.

Grandma Goldstein owned a gristmill. I remember going there. The big wheel was turning, and the water was coming and powering it. They were so poor that they didn't have outside help, so Zigmund, one of the brothers, or whoever else was there took care of it. They also had a little grocery store and a small house. On the outside, the house looked like a house in Texas, but it was very small. It had a long porch. The roof covered the porch all the way. There was a bench there. There was no big yard. There was the street in front. There were two big bedrooms (one was a living room and a bedroom and a dining room), and a big kitchen, and a very big pantry with shelves. The kitchen was separate. Once there was a little tavern, a beer hall, attached to the house. That wasn't in existence by the time we grew up. The Russians cut away half the house after the war.

The little river was right behind the house. I remember, when we slept in the same room with Grandma, we could hear the river. We would bathe in there, in little wooden tubs. Or we just sat on the rocks. And Louis and Zigmund used to catch fish. They would just lift a rock and put the net there and the fish would just swim into it. Grandma baked little fish, almost like sardines, the whole fish in a sort of ceramic pot in the oven.

Uncle Louis had a collection of stamps, big books full of stamps. Whoever had stamps, they used to give them to him. They had a balcony where Uncle Louis developed pictures. They also had a beehive behind the house, and Uncle Louis made honey. He was teaching in the one-room schoolhouse. And he was studying for the university.

Grandma Goldstein was very good-hearted and very loving. She did not have much, but she shared what she had with the poor people. Each day was a different family that came from the local village. They were all Ukrainians. One family got sour cream, one got sugar, one got bread. And they came every week. Uncle Zigmund would buy from my father's store axle grease they put on the wheels. So Grandma even gave grease to those people. That was sort of a habit. My mother used to make blueberry gin. So, a family came and knocked on the door at seven in the evening, and said their daughter was sick and she needed a little blueberry. That was a habit that everybody had.

Across from Grandma's house was a narrow gauge freight train that came to pick up the lumber. They had a coach at the end of the train, in which officials came, or some visitors. Every time the train would arrive—whether there were the officials, the managers of some plant where they manufactured the wood parts, or the engineers—they would come to the house. Grandma had, ready for them, cucumber salads, and egg salad. People came and ate, and nobody charged them anything. At that time Grandma was still OK, and everybody helped. The boys helped. Zigmund had fresh bread—he had a bakery attached to the house. He was a great baker; he learned how to bake bread in that big old-fashioned oven in Grandma's house. So when people came to eat, they had fresh bread and challah, and brown bread. And sometimes we were able to go on the train back to Svalava.

Both my father and Uncle Louis knew they were not going into the lumber business, which wasn't so good then. My father went to the school in Izvor, and then he came to Svalava to the business school. That was up to only about the age of fourteen. He learned

Figure 2

Grandmother Goldstein's House, Izvor.
Remains photographed in 1993
by Susan Goldstein

so easily that he spoke and wrote German, Hungarian, Ukrainian, and Yiddish. Uncle Louis taught in a Ukrainian school in Izvor, even after he began a correspondence course, until he left to go to Munkacs to a commercial school. It was called Kereskedelmi, which means business school, and classes were taught in Hungarian. After the business school, then he started—I don't know if he went to Prague or corresponded, but he registered and he was studying for law—law courses.

Uncle Zigmund also continued to live with Grandmother for many years. He eventually married a girl from Svalava that I knew. He had several children that I never met. He was sort of a difficult man. He had so many responsibilities. He lost his wife and children in the war. He remarried later and had a daughter and a son, who now live in Washington, D.C.

Eventually, Uncle Joseph and his family moved to Svalava, and he started two businesses. One was a bakery business with very modern equipment, which he rented. On Friday we were allowed to bring a kugel or another dish to be baked there. And on Saturday one of us would go pick it up. When Uncle Joseph moved to Svalava, Uncle Morris moved into the house next to Grandmother's house in Izvor. At this time, since Grandma was not very mobile, a niece of hers, Friede, who was divorced, came back to look after her. Friede was with my grandmother for ten years.

Oberländer Family

My father fought in the Austro-Hungarian army in the First World War, and was a prisoner of war in Italy. When he came back to Svalava, he found a matchmaker, and he met my mother and married her in 1923. My mother, Jennie (Zsenka) Oberländer, was one of nine children. The Oberländers were a very extended family. At the end of World War I, they evacuated to Hungary, to Miskolz. While they were there, my Grandmother Oberländer got influenza and she died. And my grandfather was left with nine children. At the end of the war, they all came back to Svalava, and he met a nice lady that wasn't married. His second wife, Reiszel Mayer Oberländer, was the Oberländer Grandmother I knew as a child. She never had any children herself, but she raised all my grandmother's children.

There were three boys and the rest were girls. I think the oldest was called Adolf Oberländer. He died young of pneumonia. I was close to their son Börzsi and their daughter Dorit Oberländer. Then there was a son whose name I don't remember. He was taken into the army and died in 1942 in Budapest. He was the father of my cousin, Irene Oberländer. Next came Isu Baczi who was sick with heart trouble. And he had eight children, including – Bobi, Olga, Eva, Imi, Pitu, and Isu-Bacsi [Jr].

Regina Oberländer was the oldest daughter. Her first husband was Jacobovitch and Isaac Jacobovitch was their son. Her second husband was Weiss. She lost both husbands, and she had one disabled daughter by her first husband too. They were poor, and my mother used to send packages of things to her in Szrednye. Then came my mother Jennie Oberländer. Then a daughter who died in childbirth. I don't remember her name. Her husband was Farbenblum, and they had one son, Hersi, who lost his father early to pneumonia. He now lives in Australia and has changed his name to Sam Moss. Then there were three more daughters: Lenke, Fezsi, and Manci (who was with me in Auschwitz).

Max and Jennie Goldstein Family

I later found out that, after they got married, my mother and father moved to Munkacs. My mother's sister, the aunt who died in childbirth, her husband, Farbenblum, joined my father in a business. Something to do with clothing, because a brother had a store that had all kind of accessories for sewing—buttons and thread—and another brother had children's clothing. My mother and father left Munkacs after about a year. They came back to Svalava, and my father opened up his own store, a wholesale grocery, which also had grain.

I was born on July 15, 1925 in a stone house with thick walls and narrow windows, which my parents rented. My father built a house for us next to the stone house where I was born, so I only lived there one year, but I knew it because I knew the family that

Figure 3

Max and Jennie Goldstein
at window of their Svalava home, 1930s.
One of Jennie's crocheted works hangs behind them.

built it. Melanson was their name. The next oldest to me was Tibor, who was born in August 1926. Then came Artur who was born in December 1927, then Arnold (called Nanci) who was born in 1932, then Richard, born in 1936, who died in 1939. My mother could not nurse her babies for some reason, so we had a wet nurse who came from my grandmother's village. This woman had a baby every time my mother did, and she would leave her children with her mother and come to our house. She nursed each of us as we came along. We used to give her beer and peanuts in order to increase the milk. When the nurse left, my formula was a mixture of tea and milk. That's why to this day I don't like tea and milk. [3]

Family Life

The Family Home

Our house was a long narrow rectangle. Its short sides faced the street and the back yard. The house was whitewashed brick with a steep sloped roof. The warehouse and store for my father's business were side by side at the street end, so customers could come in from the street. Next to our house on the left was the stone house where I was born. On the other side of our house was a busy inn, with a bowling alley outside with one lane under a roof. My father designed a special firewall to protect the side of our house next to the inn.

You entered the house through a gate from the street and went along a path and up a few steps to a door in a covered entry that was a little like a zigzag. We had a flower garden and flowers in the windows of the dining-living room and the bedroom. And below was a little fence holding rose trees. The only time my father gave me a slap on the face, I was at a party at a friend's house, and a good friend brought me home. And because I stood there at the gate and talked to him before I went home, my father saw it and when I came in, he slapped me. Nice girls didn't do that.

[3]   Lola's birth name was Ilona Goldstein. Her daughter Ruth notes that this wet nurse called her "Lola" from birth, the name by which she has been known to this day.

The path continued along the house to a deep backyard. We had a long lot, very long, and it ended by a little pond. We had a big high fence between our lot and the stone house that I was born in, which had a well with a roof over it and such a big backyard that people would come with their horses and park there. That's why we had the fence.

There was a one-hole outhouse in the backyard. But at night we had a pot. Back of the outhouse was also a lid to the garbage. Part of my job was to pump the water, and to carry the ashes from the stove, and the compost from the outhouse to the garden. Every year we would plant vegetables. My mother would show me how to get the potatoes and to pull the strings off the string beans. We had flowers along the side of the house. We had fruit trees—purple plums and sour cherries—and then, wild trees. My aunt had a walnut tree, and we used to go over there and pick walnuts. In the pond, there were some ducks, but we rarely went to the end where the pond was. We were afraid; the ducks would eat frogs, and we didn't like that.

Inside the back part of the house, were three large rooms next to each other—a bedroom, a living and dining room, and a kitchen with a separate pantry or storeroom. The door into the house led into a hall, with a door to the right leading into the kitchen, and a door to the left leading into the living-dining room. You crossed the living-dining room to go into the bedroom. You could enter the pantry from the kitchen, and there was a little space there for sacks of flour and other things for the store, because in the store we didn't have room for all the sacks. You entered the pantry from the kitchen, and you could go from the pantry into my father's office-store.

My mother was very creative. She designed the paint she wanted. On the bedroom ceiling we had different colors—lively stripes, yellow and blue. Above the bed, she designed a triangle with glass panes for some sides. We were able to keep little knickknacks. On the sides with the glass, we had lights inside. My mother went to the shop and told them how to make it. There were separate beds. We didn't have indoor plumbing; we had the pump

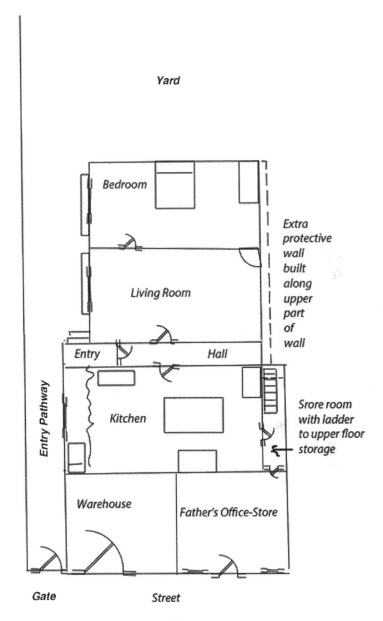

Figure 4

Plan of Max Goldstein Svalava home. Yard at back contained a pump, an outhouse, fruit trees, and a small lake. The house in which Lola was born was to the left, and an inn was to the right.

outside. We had a wardrobe where we kept linens on one side, and hanging clothes on the other, and sheets and pillowcases. My mother designed that too, and it was built to order.

There was a window in the bedroom on the garden side, and we had flowers on the window. We had rose trees outside, and we could open up the windows for the scent. There was a little stand with a washbasin in the bedroom. The side was for the towel, and the middle had a hole for the bowl and water. Underneath, there was a big pitcher and a place for the soap and sponge and brush. We had a heater, but it wasn't connected yet. So in the morning, we heated the water on the stove to put in the pitchers and had a sponge bath. The water came from the pump outside in the back yard.

There was one couch in the living room and a nice table and a second couch that was like a bed. And here, we had a big cabinet that my mother designed. It held glass things, and it had two drawers on the bottom. The dining table there was not too big, but we were four children. We had like café chairs first.

And then my mother got newer ones. We had a cream-colored tile stove in the corner. It had a little window where you could keep something warm. When we were going to give the kids their pillows, we put them against the tiles to warm them. We used timber for the stove. The wood was stored outside near where the pump was, in a big pile, and every week people came with more wood.

In the kitchen, we had a wood stove, and a big white cabinet where we kept the dishes and tablecloths. We had kosher dishes separate. We had a big table in the middle. That, too, had drawers. My mother prepared the baking on that. No sink. We didn't have running water. We had water in two pails for washing vegetables and things. We had a table, and chairs, which could move around. And the drawers had flatware. We ate in the kitchen only breakfast. In the dining room we ate only dinner. Grandma kept meat in an icebox in Izvor, but we didn't have that. We had the inn next door.

Beyond the kitchen was the large pantry or storeroom. We put meat and some other things in the pantry, because it had a cold floor, and we had a hole in the roof so the cold air could keep things cool. We even had a little window where we kept the goose liver, and an enameled container where we kept the fat.

There was an attic above the pantry area with a permanent ladder going up. There we had a little storage for fruit—pears and apples—in a box, and each pear was wrapped in tissue paper. We also had lines there where we'd hang clothes to be dried. We washed clothes in a tub in the kitchen. We brought in water from the pump outside the house in the backyard.

When I was a child, we didn't have electricity, because Svalava was too remote to bring in all the wires. By the time I went to school, we had electricity in the house. We had a chandelier—silk with ruffles—in the living room, and we had lights in the bedroom. The kitchen just got plain lights with bulbs. And we would stay up 'til one o'clock in the morning studying. We had to get up at five.

I slept on a couch in the living room. The boys slept in the kitchen near a window in the wall by the path. There was a curtain that could be pulled across, and it was kept halfway open during the day. We also had a bed in the kitchen that was a table, and the table opened up. If we had help, they slept there, or one of the children slept there. The chest for the bedding was inside there, too. Unfortunately it didn't have a mattress or sheets, just straw, but we had down pillows from the geese.

Life in Svalava

We had a pretty nice peaceful life. Czechoslovakia then was a democratic country, and we had ethnic Germans and Ukrainians that lived in our area. We had neighbors who spoke different languages. When we started talking as children, we learned four or more languages: Hungarian with our parents; Yiddish with our grandparents; German, Czech and Ukrainian with our neighbors; and Hebrew with our fellow students.

In Svalava, we had two lumber factories. The owners were Austrians. They had a big house, and the people that worked for the family used to come to our store and buy rope—we had one corner near the entrance where we had a hook with ropes. This family had a relative who established a German school in Svalava, so anyone who wanted to learn German went to school there. The rich managers bought groceries from our store. My Aunt Manci Oberländer, who lived in my grandmother's house, competed with her brother; each wanted to supply the offices for the factory with erasers and pencils, and paper products.

I had an aunt, the widow of my mother's brother who passed away, living with her children in a house overlooking the small river. They had a bakery, and bakery was a big business. My uncle on my father's side had a bakery. And another uncle from my mother's side had a bakery. There were also two little bakery outlets. So people bought rolls that had caraway seeds. And there was a German family with a grocery store – they also carried bread and rolls. Most people did, that, too, at the beginning. We had a brick oven with two doors where you could bake small things. There was a big door and we put lumber in there to heat it. And we baked for the whole week. We baked dark bread, we baked challah, we baked pastry, and cakes, everything. My mother made the dough the night before. And by the time I woke up, she had the pastry ready.

We lived near the main street and the center of town. Some people who worked in the factory were a little removed. They built their own homes. They didn't have many buildings, and they each had a little piece of ground for a garden with flowers and vegetables. One German who spoke Hungarian had a wife who was Hungarian, and they lived by the bridge in a house bigger than ours. The father was a barber. Then there were Germans that had a bakery, and the ice cream man was German. And other Germans had a small grocery store. Then, there were two stores that were run by Communists.

If we had any help, they were Ukrainian. For heavy work in the store we hired Ukrainians, and sometimes we had a Ukrainian girl help us. Every time my mother bought material for us to make dresses, she would buy for the girl too. Every time the girl would go home for the holidays, my mother would bake up a whole bunch of things for the girl to take home. There were also Gypsies who traveled. Sometimes they came on a Friday to scrub the kitchen

Figure 5

Street in Svalava, with building on far left, on site where Uncle Louis's candy store once stood. Vintage postcard, scan by Susan Goldstein.

floor when we didn't have other help. You had to be careful they shouldn't steal whatever was in their reach. Most everybody used them, but some people didn't. We were scared of them, because we were told that they would kidnap children.

When the first Model-T cars came out, these were the taxis. So if the people didn't want to take the bus or the bus was not available, you took a taxi. Everybody wanted the taxis. Across the street, where the gas station was, there was the taxi. You could take a taxi to Munkacs to do some shopping. They had clothing stores, for boys and men. There were nice fabric stores. And there was one store that was a chain called SBOR.

Max Goldstein's Business

My father had a wholesale grocery and grain business. My mother helped him in the store. In my father's office-store store, the counter was on the wall next to the pantry storeroom, so you could come here from the house. My father had a desk. On the side of the desk we had a carton with lemons—I remember standing up on it to reach. We had to clean the lamp. We didn't have electricity when I was little, my father had a lamp, and I had to clean it. There were some shelves built-in on both sides in the store, where we kept things like beans, and on both sides there were drawers. So we kept different kinds of nuts and candies in big containers, which we sold by the ounce.

We sold everything. We sold peppers, and margarine in packets. We even had axle grease. In the warehouse, my father had a grain storage that had the grain on top and the grain came down in a chute and people brought sacks to fill. We had Ukrainian men who helped with the heavy stuff. People even from the villages came in to buy. Uncle Zigmund did that. He came with a wagon and took all the things that he needed.

You know, people didn't have any money, so my father kept a little book of records, believing that eventually they would pay. There were two banks in Svalava. One was owned by Birnbaum, and one was owned by Stern. The one owned by Birnbaum was across the street from us, and many people came to borrow money.

My father went to Birnbaum. We knew the family. And—that was the biggest deal—later when I commuted to Munkacs for high school (I was 11 years old), my father gave me the papers, and I went to the bank and there was a counter so high I couldn't see the man, and they took care of the business. After that, I had to do the banking for my father, and many other people ask me to take their money. We had checks—the check was a long paper for a loan—I used to take those to the bank. When I commuted to Munkacs, people in Svalava asked me to do all kinds of errands for them: buy a new hat, or take a dress to a dressmaker, or pick up a coat or a wig.

Religion

My parents were religious, as everybody else was. My father went to shul. My mother went once a month, too. My father went to synagogue almost daily, although outwardly, he was a modern man. He didn't have a beard or anything like that. My mother always covered her head. That was the custom. Once a month we would go with my parents to synagogue. There were two synagogues in Svalava. One belonged to the oldest inhabitants. It was old and built out of wood, and there was a staircase going upstairs where the women sat. It depended on how much money you were able to give, as to where you were seated. There was a back wall where they kept the Torah, and in the center, there was a raised part where they read the Torah, and where the rabbi gave his speech. There was another synagogue, across the street from Uncle Joseph's. That was more modern and not so strict. (When we went back to visit in 1993, the Russians had a bakery in that building). On Fridays, my mother always lit candles. I think we were selling candles in the store, so she had some candles. In the beginning, we didn't have a menorah for Hanukkah. We put a piece of log in the window, and we attached candles and we sang all the songs.

We observed holidays, and we always got together with the family. We were a very close-knit larger family. In our town my father had several brothers and a sister who lived there. We were very close with them. We would visit uncles and aunts almost every weekend. Uncle Zigmund had children, and a carriage and a horse. At first he had one carriage for freight and then another for my Grandma. When she came to Svalava, we did not have a big house, but we would make room. When she came, she brought us—you know they had geese and they had feathers—so she made us brushes out of those feathers, and we used the brush to put egg yolk on bread or challah to make it shine.

On Passover, we made our own noodles. We made like crepes, and we rolled it up, and we cut it up in strips to make noodles. For the challah dough, we would make also a platform, and we would mix cottage cheese with egg and sugar and put it on top. It was like a pizza. It was open, and it was sweet. And on Passover, when we came back from the schul, we would stop at Uncle Joseph's and try their potato latkes. Then we went to Aunt Rose's house, and then to our house, tasting latkes everywhere. On Purim, it was the custom to see who had the biggest collection of pastries. We had special dishes for the holidays. We had cups with blue polka dots on them. Even in Izvor, in that little town and that little house, they had a separate set of dishes for Passover. There was no basement. They had a big pantry, with shelves on both sides. The pantry was bigger than the kitchen. I remember eating there matzo, and potato pancakes. Potato pancakes were a big thing.

Relatives

We visited my Oberländer grandparents every Friday night, and the extended family we met either in shul, or they didn't live too far. Grandfather Oberländer died in 1936. I was a child. I could remember some of the festival dinners at my Grandfather's house. And when my grandfather died, they brought special dishes down.

I was Grandmother Oberländer's favorite grandchild, so I spent a lot of time with her. She slept in an old-fashioned bed and she couldn't sleep with another person, so she put two chairs together with a pillow on them and that's where I slept, next to her bed. She would take me on vacation to see her family and that was very nice. She was the one who said I should go to a Jewish girls' school. Later on, when I commuted to high school in Munkacs, she would have a candle in the window and say a prayer for me as I traveled by train to the next town, that I should have a safe journey, going and coming back.

My mother had several sisters. When I was born, two of them were not married yet and they stayed very close to us. One of my aunts was a beautiful sewer. She sewed all my dresses. All of them had difficult lives. Only my Aunt Manci survived the war. She has a daughter, Magda Grin, who now lives in Staten Island.

Daily Life

My parents tried to give us whatever they could. We went to school. My mother was very active. She used to get magazines from Vienna. I don't know how she got them, whether they came by mail. Fashion magazines. And stories. One was translated into Hungarian. It was Delibab. She designed her own clothes, and then had it made. And my father had fancy coats, lined with fur and with fur collars. My mother never had a fur coat. She just had a coat with a Persian wool collar.

We all had chores to do. We had a flower garden. We had a vegetable garden. We all had to help with jobs. We had brass doorknobs and brass handles on the windows, and every Thursday we had to polish them. We had to wash the wooden floors. We had to wash clothes by hand and hang outside on a line. We didn't have washing machines. But we survived. My mother made sure that I learned to do things. I was the only girl, so besides going to school, my mother taught me how to sew, how to knit, how to crochet, and how to mend socks for my brothers. If there was a hole in the sock, we didn't just go out and buy a new pair. We fixed them. There was the custom in every family that you had to prepare a dowry, embroidered sheets and pillowcases and tablecloths. I had to do that. My mother also taught me how to garden.

Sometimes, we would grow our own potatoes. Then we picked them, and peeled them, and grated them, and dried them. For wintertime, we had a cellar—not under out house, but under the neighbor's house, the house where I was born. There was a box

Figure 6

Max and Jennie Goldstein Family at entry to Svalava home.
Back: Jennie, Lola, Max. Middle: Tibor, Artur.
Front: Arnold (Nancsi).

with sand, and buried in the sand, we would keep celery roots and carrots and onions, those we didn't keep in the house.

My mother was a great gardener. She grew roses. And she was a good baker and a wonderful cook. She taught me how to how to cook—how to make pasta from scratch, not in a machine, and how to clean a chicken. Her mother died in the First World War, but my mother learned cooking from her stepmother. She was a good cook. She married off all the children: all the weddings were in the backyard, and they had such equipment big pans for cooking and coffee cake. We had four complete sets of dishes: dairy and meat for everyday, and dairy and meat for Passover. (We didn't have much for dairy on Passover; we had like bowls for cereal.)

We made sauerkraut in a big crock. Making sauerkraut was a family affair. There was the blade, and we put it on two stools, and we sat there, and you pushed the cabbage back and forth, and it fell on a sheet. Then we put it in a big barrel with salt, and we had just a few grape vines, so we put the green grapes in there to give it taste. And then we put a piece of bread on it to ferment it and we put a rock on the lid. We left it about a month, before we were able to eat it. It was delicious, crunchy sauerkraut. We would make stuffed cabbage and have sauerkraut with it. In the middle of the house, we had an opening like a shaft that was open to the fresh air, and the sauerkraut was stored in the barrel all winter.

Then we had geese. We bought a goose. I'm not sure who had the geese to sell, but they came door to door and we would buy a goose. When we had our goose, we would sit on the floor with our legs crossed and force feed the goose so it would get very fat. We kept it in a little cage. I don't remember where the cage was – probably outdoors in summertime. We took the goose to a shochet to kill it in a kosher way. We'd take the down and the feathers. And then we made goose fat. We kept a goose every week or so. We had a huge table, and we had a holding tank of collecting goose fat. We kept that until it was filled. In the goose fat, we would put cooked goose liver, and it kept fresh in the goose fat. We sautéed it with onion, and we used to slice it and eat it with mashed potatoes and sautéed onion on the mashed potatoes. That was a Friday lunch.

On Friday we didn't want to have a big lunch, because we had a Friday night dinner.

People also would sell chickens, and I remember they stopped at the store and they ruffled the feathers so they could see how much fat there was. We made Friday night dinner—chicken soup, and chicken and mashed potatoes. We did, sometimes, baked potatoes, but that wasn't with the Friday night meal. It was a dairy meal. We made goulash. We made stuffed cabbage a lot. We used a lot of beans. There was a rabbi, and he had a yeshiva. So these Orthodox boys would come, and they would sleep in one place and eat every day in another house. They ate at Grandma Oberländer's house too. And there was a joke going around that every day they would get bean-sick in different houses.

Everybody made gefilte fish. My mother made it not the way many other women did. My mother had the whole fish. She would cut off the head. She then carefully lifted the skin without cutting it. She took out the whole skeleton with the flesh on it. Then she would chop up the flesh with eggs, onions, and matzo meal, chop it real fine, and stuff it back in the skin. Gefilte means stuffed. Then she would boil it with carrots, celery, and onions, and sometimes the head of the fish. She would carefully life out the whole stuffed fish, put it on a platter and slice it.

And we used to make green peppers stuffed with cabbage, in a jar. (I didn't eat it, I never liked peppers.) And we had the sauerkraut. My mother cooked a lot with the sauerkraut. Cabbage she used to make. She also made cholent.[4] A cholent is made up of beans, barley, and meat in a big pot and baked in the oven. After we no longer had the oven we would take it to the bakery to put in the oven for pickup on Saturday. Besides the cholent dish, we made a kugel out of potatoes with eggs and onions, and it was so crispy.

In summertime I had to help with the canning. Canning was a big deal. There were no canned goods to be had. You couldn't

---

4   Cholent is a traditional Jewish stew. It is usually simmered overnight Friday for 12 hours or more, and eaten for lunch on Shabbat (the Sabbath). (Wikipedia)

buy them anywhere. My mother taught me how to can fruit and vegetables. She used to buy big quantities and I would stand and scrub cucumbers, and sterilize the jars and bottles. She used to make tomato juice and put it in wine bottles, and put wax to seal it—cork first and then the wax. We made raspberry juice and pickles and tomatoes, and all kinds of things. We also had a plum tree, and we would make spiced plums. They were very good. We had our own compote—you know, spicy. We put in grapes and wine, so it was a job. We had a small garden, where we grew beans and radishes and cucumbers and green onions. And we made pickles from cucumbers. We also had to help go get walnuts, and get the nuts out of the shells. Summer was a hard time. Canning was a big deal. We couldn't go to the river to swim until we had done our jobs with the canning. We lived off that in the winter.

My father had to get up very early to be at the store, and he ate at his desk. I used to go, when I wasn't in school, to get fresh rolls, some with poppy seeds, some with caraway seeds. He liked them with butter and jam. And he liked the milk—we boiled the milk and it created a coating—he liked that for his coffee. (I don't like that.) I ate on the go.

Our town had two rivers. When we were children we would go and bathe there. I never learned how to swim. My parents had a friend, an elderly man, and he tried to teach me. He took me and let go of me in the deepest part of the water and I started drowning, and my mother was on the shore screaming. That fear sealed my swimming. To this day I am petrified of water. I go in a pool that is four feet deep and I get scared.

Winter brought snow. The snow fell December first and didn't melt until April first. In winter we went sledding. There was a main street and it curved. This is where the river was, and my aunt lived there. And her brother owned a mill across the river. You went across the little river on a bridge. We went past the mill and up. We had a high sled, and once I was sledding in the mountains with the brother of a friend. We went down and at the bottom there was a sort of rock covered with snow. So we up-jumped, overturned. We had a skating rink. There was a building where we exercised and they had the skating rink outside. You went inside to warm up. We had the skates you fasten to your shoes. My brothers skated. And I was a very good skater. And my cousin skated, who is now ninety-two and is in Los Angeles. There was also skiing in the mountains. I was too young to ski, but Aunt Magda, she skied. And Uncle Louis skied.

School

Czech School in Svalava

In Svalava, we had school only up to middle school. The beginning of my schooling was in a Czech public school. I went for two years there. They had Ukrainian and Czech schools. I went to the Czech school. In the Czech schools, the subjects were in Czech. This was an old school, but when I started first grade, there was a brand new school that the Czechs built. The building was very modern. There were eight grades, but sometimes there were two classes of first grade, two classes of fourth grade. It was a big school. When you came into the hallway there was a wire thing, and they had pegs where you could hang your coats in a row. You could change your shoes and boots. They closed that in with the wire screen. You could see in, but they didn't want people to steal.

When we came in, we had classwork first and then some exercises. The classes weren't very long. Sometimes we had the same teacher, sometimes other teachers. There weren't that many, so they would have to share the duties. I learned to read there. Mathematics was important. The teacher demonstrated. If you knew the answer you raised your hand. There weren't many books. There were only a few. They would copy books from the library. They did that in the Czech, and in the Hebrew School, too, because they didn't have any books. We would have to write something and then the teacher would take it home and he would go over it and mark it. The writing was mostly geography and history—to learn where you are, about Svalava and the surrounding towns, because some children came from those towns to the school. We did writing, line after line, the lines repeating, writing from memory.

There was a gymnasium where you had to have special shoes. We did calisthenics. And they had a ladder you climbed. And they had more. They had "horses" we jumped over. We played volleyball both inside and out. Half of the class played the other half. I remember that we had pochodove teaching—it means exercise. The war was starting already, so we had to go and march outside to gear ourselves up. Walk, walk, walk, in case you have to leave the house. We got home about 12. So we went probably from 8 in the morning to 12 or 1 o'clock.

At home we had a piano. I took piano lessons from a German. He was more than strict. If you couldn't do the chords, he put a pencil here [gesturing weaving the pencil between fingers]. And if you didn't know your lesson, he would put a coin on the floor and you had to kneel on it. He was a Nazi, and when Hitler came to power, he left his family, he left all of his students, and he went off to join Hitler. He never came back.

Svalava Hebrew Day School

Before anti-Semitism started, my father's business had all kinds of customers, Jews and non-Jews. Then the townspeople were throwing rocks at us. In 1933, as soon as we heard that Hitler had become Chancellor of Germany, my father, along with several other parents, decided to start a Hebrew Day School. They rented a room in a small apartment house. It was in three different locations. In those days they built apartment after apartment with a long back yard. So then they rented a room that was near the long back yard so we could go to the outhouse and do sports. They began with some sports.

In the one room, there were six grades with one teacher, Mrs. Keliner, who taught mostly the higher grades. There was also one volunteer. In the Hebrew grade school, that teacher taught math, geography, and all the subjects. We heard what the first-graders learned and the fourth-graders, and all the grades. There were two Birnbaum sisters—Elisabeth (Elza) and Piri—who used to come and teach us homemaking. They taught us how to cook. There was no stove, they taught us just the theory. They taught us how to embroider. They taught us how to sew, how to make little pillows. They showed us this is a pillow and this is a pillow cover. Some covers were plain cloth and some were embroidered.

In our kitchen at home, we would put pictures made out of white cotton and red embroidery. My mother showed us how to do all the intricate things in embroidery. You know, you pull out threads and make a little ladder almost. I was the only girl in my family, so besides going to school, in summertime, I had to learn how to sew. My mother had some designs, and we prepared some for my dowry. Again, you couldn't go to the river until you did some embroidery.

Even though I went to Hebrew Day School and understood what I read in the prayers, my Grandmother Oberländer said, "You've got to learn the old-fashioned way." So I had to go to a Jewish girls' school in the afternoon. I had to learn to pray the old-fashioned way. All three of my brothers went to a Cheder, a religious school. Cheder in Hebrew means "a room." That's where they had their religious upbringing. Sometimes the students went to this Cheder early in the morning before regular school, and sometimes they went after school.

We couldn't leave when the Germans started marching across Europe. We didn't have any connections. We didn't have any money. Where would we go? You know people in Western Europe, they had businesses, they had money, they had connections. They were able to escape. We couldn't. It was a small town, only 10,000 people. And we had neighbors who were Ukrainian and German and Hungarian. Among the people I know, nobody was hiding, nobody. The place was too small, and we were too known. Everybody knew each other.

Figure 7

Pupils at the
Hebrew Day
School,
with their teacher
and his wife.
The name Márta
was printed
mistakenly
without the accent
over the "a."
Photograph
taken
in the late 1930s.

Figure 8

Group of
students from
Svalava who
attended the
Munkacs Hebrew
Gymnasium.
Lola is standing
second from
right.
Photograph
taken in
Svalava, in
December 1942.

Part II: The Troubles Begin

Munkacs Hebrew Gymnasium

I went to the Hebrew Day School in Svalava from grade 3 to 5. We then had a choice whether to go to high school after 4 grades or 5. High school was for eight years because junior and senior high schools were combined. We didn't have a high school in our town. The Czechs had what was called a four-year Commerce School after grade school. I didn't go to that. I went to the Hebrew high school (or Gymnasium) in Munkacs. At that time there were only two Hebrew high schools in Czechoslovakia. The other was in Ungvar, the capital of a section of Carpathia. It was not as good a school. The Munkacs Hebrew Gymnasium was very famous. It was the best Hebrew school in Europe. Our principal, Dr. Kugel, was a member of the Czech Parliament. I went to school with his daughter. He emigrated to Israel in 1939, and became mayor of Cholon, a town outside of Tel Aviv. He was so well known they named a street after him.

Structure and Curriculum

There were about four hundred students in our high school. We were told that the stones were brought from Jerusalem to build the high school. I don't know if it's true. It was a very good school, and attracted teachers from all over Europe. We had very good teachers. I attended the regular classes. In Hebrew high school, during the Czech Republic, we had different teachers who came to our classroom for each subject and we studied everything in Hebrew. We had every subject—language, literature, geography, geometry, math, chemistry, and art.

We studied several languages: Czech, Hebrew, English, Latin, and later, Hungarian. At our school, things were difficult. We had a small library, not many books, and they weren't publishing any books. So, in certain subjects, the books were mimeographed on sort of brownish paper, in Hebrew. The typewriters were not very good, and the printing wasn't very good.

Each subject was a class. One principal taught a class on Israel. The Bible we studied as literature, not because we were religious (as a matter of fact, in Israel today every student memorizes the Bible—not the whole thing, but many sections—and they can quote a lot of things from the Bible). In mathematics, we used Arabic numerals. I did not like mathematics, because we didn't have good teachers. They were so impatient, especially one who became the principal of the school. He was the third principal, Mr. Rubin. He was a mathematician, but he did not know how to teach us. He got so frustrated that he did not know what to do. Mr. Rubin also taught chemistry. He demonstrated experiments at his desk.

We had one student who was not Jewish. He was of German descent, and because the Czechs didn't like the Germans, some people were not nice to him at the Czech school. He wanted to leave the Czech school and came to the Munkacs Gymnasium. His father was a train engineer, and he said to the principal who taught chemistry, "Would you do me a favor and take my son?" They usually didn't take any non-Jews, but they took him. This boy was very smart—in about a year, he learned Hebrew.

Another principal was from Slovakia. His name was Morvai, which means he was from Morova. He was with the military, and he was an artist. He hung charcoal paintings in the hallway at school. He had some pictures of people and some with the mountains and gardens. And he taught us art. They provided us with some paper. I remember he taught us a winter scene, and I remember my mountain—I didn't know how to do it. It looked like the figures were falling off. This teacher is also the one who taught us how to burn on velvet to make pictures. He taught us how to do pillows with velvet and designs. I don't remember exactly how, but it was something done with fire. They took him to slave labor. He never came back.

We had to know our subjects because we had finals, and they were very strict in grading. We had such a time. I remember one time studying until one o'clock in the morning. I couldn't read well, the words were so blurry, and I would rub my eyes. I didn't realize, but I was told I couldn't see. I needed glasses, but I didn't know it. When I got to the Gymnasium, that need was established. And you had to pay for it too.

School Life

In the morning, I ate on the go. I would get up at five o'clock in the morning and have a quick breakfast. My mother cooled my coffee or cocoa by pouring it from cup to cup, and that was important to make the train when I went to school in Munkacs. The coffee was a quarter cup of chicory and the rest was milk. I would have just a piece of bread with butter or something. We didn't have cereal. The only cereal that my mother would cook was oatmeal, or cream of wheat. For lunch I would take bread and butter, sometimes with jam or goose fat. We had no cafeteria in the school, and I didn't come home for lunch. I had to take lunch with me. My brothers were in school in Svalava. They came home for lunch.

I took the train at six o'clock and didn't get back until three thirty. I was eleven when I started the train trip in 1936. We passed on the train a castle that belonged to the Hapsburgs. The man who was in charge of the castle when the Austrians came there, was Schönborn-Buchheim, and he went to business school with my father. So he would bring us sometimes pears from the surroundings of the castle. For a time, my two brothers joined me at school in Munkacs. We commuted to school by train every day.

With no cafeteria at school, at lunchtime we would walk in the corridors, eating our sandwich and trying to memorize our next day's studies in literature or history. The custodian's wife had a little candy store, and if we had a few cents we could buy a candy bar. That same lady boiled some milk, and for five cents we could get a cup of milk to drink. Sometimes it was scorched and had that bitter taste. In spite of all this, we had to pay tuition, and sometimes we had to pay more tuition for some of the children who couldn't afford it, so they could go to school, and sometimes we would pay for the milk for them, too. Even with all the difficulties it was a very good school.

In our first year in high school we would look up at the eighth-graders. To us they were "grown-ups". We had a sort of big yard, and in the summertime we would go out and just socialize. We had such camaraderie in high school. We would visit classmates and study together. We went to school six days a week, with Saturday off. On Saturdays we would get together, and sometimes a teacher would like to get together with the students and sing songs, or have political discussions. We used to go out and have picnics. There was a spring holiday, Tu B'Shevat, toward the end of the school year. We would go into the mountains and different classes would meet there. We had to walk. Imagine eight classes, which started out in different directions, and about let's say 10 to 15 kilometers away, we would meet in a clearing on top of a mountain and we would have a picnic and dancing and singing. It was just wonderful.

Life Changes

Grandmother Esther Goldstein's Death

Grandma Goldstein died in 1938 at age 70. My parents had gone to Kosice, a town in Czechoslovakia, because there was a fair, and my Uncle Louis stayed with us and took care of the business while they were away. Unfortunately, my grandmother passed away that day, and they had to return before they could finish. I was too young to go to the cemetery. It wasn't in the little village, Izvor, but in the next town. Grandma had 60 grandchildren, and many great-grand children, the oldest of whom were in the United States, because they were descendants of the oldest three brothers who went early to America.

Trouble Brews

In 1938 the Germans occupied western Czechoslovakia (or the Sudeten) and things changed. Svalava was occupied by the

Hungarians, who were allies of the Germans. They marched into Munkacs in spring of 1938, but they stayed there; they didn't march any further. So we were cut off. We got food from Slovakia through the mountains. Anti-Semitism increased in 1939, when Germany occupied first Austria and then Poland. And it was getting worse and worse.

We tried to listen to news—to England, to London—but that was against the law. If they caught you, you went into jail. So we tried to find out; we knew about the laws against Jews, Hitler's laws, but a lot we didn't know. The newspapers wouldn't write about much. Kristallnacht, we never heard about. They closed down our school. In a period of one month, we had four different flags. First it was Czechoslovakia. Then it was Ukraine. Then it was Hungary. Then it was Germany.

After the Hungarians took over, we started school again in 1939, in the fall. I couldn't start until spring of 1940, so I lost one year. I had to drop down a grade because I missed it. Very few remained of the old teachers. They brought in knowledgeable Hungarian teachers. The Hungarian teachers were nice, but everything changed. We had new subjects—we had to learn Hungarian culture, Hungarian history, and Hungarian literature. We had an English teacher that was born in Slovakia and was Jewish. She went to school in Oxford. She was small, and when she came, she stood up on the table and she said, "The pepper is small but strong." And she said, "I will not talk to you in any other language but English." That's how we learned.

In 1940, a schoolteacher and his children were given permission to go to Israel (the permissions were called certificates). And the teacher's wife—my father used to date her before they were married—and we were friends, and I went to school with the teacher's daughter. When I visited them before they left, the mother said, "You know, we have these papers. We have two children. We can add another child to it, and maybe take you with us." When I came home and told my father, he said, "Go ask your mother." My mother said, "You are going to leave us?" So I didn't go.

We went to school until 1942. When things were getting bad, my brothers no longer took the train every day with me. They were students by correspondence. They studied the books at home, and then went and took the exams. That was when there was the epidemic of meningitis. We didn't know who brought it, whether the Hungarians brought it or soldiers. At school, when we went on our holiday excursions, they now made us march to and from the mountains.

Nearby the train tracks to school, there was the castle owned by the Schönborn-Buchheim Austrian family, who were related to the Hapsburgs. (These counts owned hunting castles.) We had only a small infirmary, so the castle became a hospital for the epidemic. There were people all over the floor. They didn't have beds, or blankets, no pillows. That is where my youngest brother, Richard, was diagnosed with meningitis in 1939. He was then moved to a hospital for contagious diseases, where he was kept for just a short time. There was nothing they could do for him, so they sent him home and he died soon after.

Jews Taken Away, Jewish Businesses Shut

Up until 1942, we still had food, and my father still had merchandise in the store. And he sold grain that they took to the villages and ground. We still went to shul. We had a Midrash, which was a little more progressive. And we had a synagogue more conservative, Bet Midrash. My parents belonged to this Midrash. And we still celebrated holidays as long as we could.

In 1942, The Hungarians went door to door asking for citizenship papers. People, even though they were born there, if they couldn't prove and show their papers, they were deported. Mothers, fathers, children and grandparents, were all taken away. If you couldn't prove your citizenship, they took you. They split up families. I knew one family whose father with a daughter were visiting someplace else. They took his wife even though she was born in Czechoslovakia, but her husband was of Polish descent. They took her and the two other children at home. We knew that they were taken to Poland, but we didn't know where and why. We never heard about concentration camps. Even in 1942 we didn't know where those people were taken. That's when practically half the Jewish population was taken, and a whole transport went to Auschwitz. We didn't know where they went. We never heard from them again.

In Svalava, Magda Blaufeld went on the train with me to the Gymnasium, and we became friends. She used to go to Uncle Louis's candy store in Svalava, and she became acquainted with him. On March 29, 1942, they were married at Magda's home. They had beautiful flowers and a lot of fruit trees. And they had a tall fence. I remember going to the railroad station, and passing the boundary of their home where they had a big German shepherd dog that I was scared of. Magda and Louis's happiness didn't last long.

The Hungarians and the Germans were allies. Horthy[1] had made a pact with the Germans, "We'll give you slave laborers, but don't touch the Jews." But shortly after Uncle Louis and Aunt Magda were married, the Hungarians expanded their search and took away all the able-bodied Jewish men for slave labor. Uncle Louis was conscripted as an officer in the Czech army, so Magda and Louis were separated. He was captured and taken for slave labor. Many of those taken for slave labor worked digging trenches on the fronts of the war. Eventually most of them ended up in Siberia, including my Uncle Louis, my Uncle Zigmund, my Uncle David, and Manci's husband. Life was pretty tough after that.

[Lola's family was caught in the worsening trauma. Her Uncle Louis Goldstein wrote of his experiences in his memoirs. The following excerpts are from text provided by his daughter Julie Ellis, and are included with her permission:][2]

"Starting in 1939, all young Jewish men were forced to work in Hungarian slave labor camps for several months each year. In

---

1   Miklós Horthy was Regent of Hungary from 1920-1944.

2   The official Hungarian name for this "duty" was "labor battalion" or "Arbeitskommando." Note that to Louis and his companions, the camps were "Hungarian slave labor camps."

1939, I was in a camp for a few weeks in Munkacs. In 1940, I spent a few months in a camp in Yugoslavia. In 1941, I worked for a few months in a lumber camp in Csernoholova."

There were no young men left. Who was left? Old women, and women with children. My father was too old to be taken for slave labor, even though he was only 46 years old. My mother was 41. As Jews, after 1942, we wore yellow stars. The authorities took all Jewish people's business licenses away. They took my father's business license away, and locked up his store full of merchandise. We asked what would happen to it. They confiscated it, took it away, and said, "This is in lieu of the taxes for next 50 years."

We didn't have any food. We were given rations for sugar and bread, and once in a while for meat. So if we had more sugar than we needed, we would take it to the farms and barter it for eggs, or for milk, and once in a while for a chicken. We made things get by. If my mother would cook a chicken, she would eat the feet and one of us would eat the head, you know scrape out the brains and cook it, so my father and the other children could get the legs. The breast was chopped up and made into "hamburger," because we didn't like the dry white meat. My mother also made false gefilte fish. She would chop up the chicken meat and cook it as though it would be fish. We had to be inventive.

Max Goldstein Imprisoned

My father did business with a Romanian cheese company. They shipped, by rail, barrels of cheese like Greek feta cheese, and goat, and lamb cheese. They would ship that into the forest for the lumberjacks. The lumberjacks would eat that and make a bonfire. That brought us a little money. And after they took our license away, the connection was still there. But the cheese company made a mistake one day, and instead of shipping the cheese to the forest, they sent the cheese to our house.

One of our ethnic German neighbors (the Schläger boy) reported my father to the police, who arrested him, because he wasn't allowed to run a business after they had taken his license

Figure 9

Group of men
with two boys.
Taken in Svalava,
December 1942.
Lola's Uncle David
is 5th from right
in the row of men.
Lola's cousin David
(Uncle Jospeh's
son, known as
Dudi) is 8th from
the right, the last
man in the group.

away. They put my father in the bottom of the police station in a cellar like a dungeon, where winter vegetables were kept. He just sat crouched on the ground. He couldn't even stand up. My mother packed up some food, and I took it in a bucket to give it to him. The ceiling was so low that he could just crouch. I gave him the food, and the policeman said, "Enough, enough. Shut the door on him." It broke my heart. I can still see his face to this day. What did my mother do? She asked some of the relatives and collected some money. A cousin of mine who was a lawyer went to Budapest and hired another lawyer to get him out of jail.

Changes at the Munkacs Hebrew Gymnasium

I attended the Hebrew Gymnasium for 6 years. Then the Germans came, and they were situated in the school too. So there was no place for us to study. There was a funeral home. They didn't prepare bodies there; they just made arrangements for the cemetery and the burial. The school decided to move there. There was a big hall, and they put mattresses to separate it into spaces for the different grades. But you could still hear the sounds from one class to another. Shortly after that, the train stopped because the Army needed the trains. We went to school in two shifts, half of the school in the morning and half in the afternoon. I had continued commuting every day until the civilian trains stopped running. Then I would stay with different families so I could continue to go to school. Whoever went to Munkacs from Svalava took along food for me in a sort of carrier with a handle on it, similar to containers the Chinese use. I stayed with three different families. Then, at graduation, they brought a priest who spoke Hebrew, and could supervise graduation that year. I didn't quite make it because I had lost the time when the school was closed down in 1938-1939.

Prisoners going to their barracks after registration.
1. Martha Junger nee Birnbaum from Szolyva – survived
2. Dora Birnbaum Martha and Emil's mother
3. Emma Gottesman nee Birnbaum – survived
4. Gita Liberman – survived
   other possibility: Etus (Edith) Moze nee Talmanovics
5. Agi Rooiner Katz
6. Minica Balacsk Gottesman – survived
7. Maid: Birnbaum – survived
8. Rici Feldman

אסידות בדרכן אל הבלוקים לאחר שסיימו את תהליך הרישום
1. מרחה יונגר לבית בירונבאום מסוליבה. היא שרדה
2. דורה בירונבאום. אמן של מרחה וארנה
3. ארנה גוטסמן לבית בירונבאום. היא שרדה
4. גיטה ליברמן. היא שרדה
ויהי אבשרי אחר: אחעש [אסתר] מוהס לבית ולמנוביץ
5. אגי רובינר לבית כץ
6. מיניץ בן צהולר לבית גוטסמן. היא שרדה
7. מייד: בירונבאום. היא שרדה
8. רוזי פלדמן

86

Figure 10

Neighbors from Svalava in Auschwitz, 1944.
Photocopy of page from an album of photos taken, by a
German officer, of prisoners in Camp 5 at Auschwitz-Birkenau.
This was Lola Goldstein's area of the camp,
but she is not in the picture.

Part III: Holocaust and Postwar Chaos

In 1941 and 1942 the Hungarians started taking the Jews for slave labor. Our schools were closed again. We still couldn't leave. Before we were taken away, my father bought a bathtub. And we had a heater, heating water in pots and pans, and soap. But we didn't use it very long, because we were taken away.

There was a Jewish slave labor camp stationed about 3 kilometers from our town. The labor camp was temporary. As the front was moving ahead, they kept moving. They were there just for a week or two. I don't know where they stayed, whether they had tents or they put them in homes. They had to do whatever dirty work there was. For Sabbath, we would invite some of the Jewish boys to have dinner with us. Even though we didn't have much, we shared it. Later on these boys went to the front, and they were digging ditches and fixing the railroads so the train should run. It's so funny what an organization the Nazis had. From Germany to Hungary, they could schedule the trains—when they should run and take the people away.

Svalava Jews Taken
Gathering the Jews

At the beginning of 1944, the Germans marched into Svalava. They occupied part of every Jewish home. They came to our house, and we had to move into our bedroom—the whole family. We put a stove in there, and cooked, ate, and slept, all six of us, in that one room. We had German officers and their office was the rest of the house. The officer came in the evenings, and we never knew whether this was our last day. I don't recall whether my mother was able to light Shabbos candles or not. There weren't many Fridays after that.

Finally we were taken away. We were given no reason, only that the Germans had lists. There were townspeople who were ethnic Germans, and they gave the officials all the information. They told them, "This house is a Jewish family. This house is Jewish." There was a lumberyard, across from street from my Oberländer grandmother's house. The family participated in the all the synagogues. The owner had some authority. He had a list on paper of all the Jewish people, and he was trying to protect some of the Jews. They took him last, but they took him, nevertheless.

When we were taken away, it was the day after Passover in April, 1944. We had two hours to get ready, to gather all we could carry, and walk to the synagogue. The people who came to order us to leave were local customers of my father. Now, they gave us two hours to get ready. We grabbed whatever we could. A blanket, a coat, shoes. We didn't travel much, so we didn't have many suitcases or backpacks.

Before the war we had good relations with our neighbors. Now some ethnic Germans who owned ice cream parlors, and often bought sugar, salt, and other ingredients from my father to make their ice cream and pastries, came to our house and said we should give them our jewelry. They promised to save it for us, for when we come back. We knew they would not do that. My mother had silver candlesticks and silver bowls, and we had to leave it all.

The day we left was the day after Passover, and that year it was before Easter. We didn't have any more matzo left, and we didn't yet have bread. So we went to some Germans neighbors named Schläger, whom we had considered friends. They owned the barbershop, and all the Jews went to that one and only barbershop. They also had pigs and cows, and were well off. The mother was Hungarian, and they had several daughters. One daughter was my mother's age, and the two of them were very friendly. Before the troubles began, on Christmas, my mother would make fondant, the white candy, and wrap it in fancy foil to hang on their Christmas tree, and we were invited to see the tree. One son was an idealist who went to Israel in the 1930s, and never came home. I don't know if he converted to Judaism. We never heard from him.

When the war began, we had to cover the windows with dark paper so the bombers shouldn't see the lights. Now if a little piece of paper came off, the Schlägers would report, us and we had to pay the fines. The Schläger's son was also the one who reported my father when they saw the cheese being delivered to our house. At this time, Christians had a custom of baking big braided bread, challahs, which they would put in a basket and take in a procession, flags waving, to the Church at Easter and bless with holy water. I knew they had all kinds of baked goods, so despite everything, I went over to the Schläger's house, and I explained to them that we didn't any have any matzo or bread, and asked would they give us some bread. They slammed the door in my face.

Transport to Munkacs Kalush Ghetto

When we left our homes, we were gathered in the Svalava synagogue, and we slept one night on the floor there, with men and women and everybody. We didn't have nightclothes—just our own clothes. The next day, they put us in boxcars and sent us to a ghetto in Munkacs, the town where I went to school. When we were taken in the boxcars, some of the Jewish boys from the labor camp near town tried to bring us bread, but the Germans pushed them away, so they could not give us the bread. The ghettos in Munkacs were in the drying sheds of brick factories. There were two brick factories in that town. Half the Jewish population was taken to one brick factory and half to the other. Our ghetto was named Kalush. In the factory where we were, there were two permanent buildings, and several sheds where they dried the bricks. Each of these had just a roof and four posts holding up the roof. They must have once had shelves to put the bricks on. But when we came, there were no shelves, no walls, no doors. They put us together in one of these sheds—men and women and children—on the bare ground. We were just body-to-body. We used what blankets we had brought to create walls, to cover the bare ground, and to help us be covered. We didn't know what to do—whether to use the blankets that we brought to create a wall or to keep us warm.

Aggi Birnbaum happened to be in the same brick factory when I was. Also In the group, there was a classmate of mine whose mother was in the United States with the father remaining in Czechoslovakia. They beat him daily to tell why the mother was in the United States, and what contact he had with her. The father perished, but two sisters survived and lived in Florida. One of them is such a recluse she doesn't want to meet anybody. We had a reunion and the older sister came, but the younger one never wanted to come. You know it leaves an impression on you when you see your father being beaten.

The conditions in the ghetto in Munkacs were just impossible. We were given a bowl of indescribable soup and one piece of bread a day. We were sleeping on the bare ground – strangers next to each other. There was nothing to do. In one of the little buildings, they made an infirmary. They had blind people there, and people with TB. We were given a few potatoes, so a group of us young girls volunteered to give the sick people in the infirmary something to eat. We found a little kitchen and we tried to cook some potatoes for the sick people.

When The Germans took us into the ghetto, the German train engineer, whose son had been accepted to study at the Munkacs Hebrew Gymnasium, came to the principal of the Gymnasium after it was displaced into the funeral home, this was the second or third principal already after the one who taught chemistry and had accepted the engineer's son as a pupil with us. The German train engineer now said that he and his family would pick up the principal's son and hide him. And they did that. And this boy remained in Hungary, and got in touch with us after the war. He had become an engineer in Hungary.

Transport to Auschwitz

After four weeks being in the brick factory in Munkacs, little by little, in groups, they put us in boxcars again and shipped us to Auschwitz. We knew bits of information about what was happening. We knew that the Germans made people gather in a field to dig their own graves, stand there, and then be shot. We knew of beating. We knew of starvation. But we didn't know about death camps. When we were leaving the ghetto, an old friend of my family said, "My dear, don't worry about it. You know this is 1944. It isn't 1940 or 1942 when they were so brutal. Hitler won't dare do in 1944 what he did in 1942. They are not going to do any more now, because they know that the Russians are within kilometers of us." You could hear the bombers come. And yet they grabbed us and took us. There were some people I knew who were hiding in the woods. They put out a price for their heads. They found where they were hiding, and went and caught them and shipped them to Auschwitz.

They took us, one transport after another transport. As we were herded on the way to the boxcars, the officers would shoot into the air and say, "You'd better give us all your jewelry or else you'll be killed." We didn't know where the train was headed, but then we started seeing Polish names on the railroad stations, and we knew we were across the border. So people were desperate, and they thought that rather than give everything to the Germans, they would dig a little hole on the road with their shoe heel, and bury the jewelry in the road. The trip was horrible, horrible. We were so crowded. I can't remember where my three brothers sat, but I remember sitting on a duffel bag or some suitcases between my mother and my father. In the boxcars, we had no food, no water, no sanitation. We had one piece of bread for three days in a boxcar. They had one big zinc bowl to relieve ourselves, but you never could get to it, there were so many people. One woman gave birth to a child. Another woman went berserk. People were screaming. Some people told me that in other cars some people were dying. This went on for three days and three nights. My father told me, "No matter what they do to you—they can take everything away from you, but the little education you've got, they can't take away."

Auschwitz-Birkenau

Arrival at Auschwitz

We finally arrived in Auschwitz on May 22, 1944. We could see burning chimneys and flames coming out of chimneys. And we asked some of the old prisoners who helped us get off the train, "What is that?" And they said, "That's a bakery." These were the old inmates that were there a long time. They said, "Don't worry about the suitcases. Just jump off and walk." Later we found out it was really the flames coming out from the crematorium, from the ovens they had to cremate the corpses. We thought we were taken to a camp where the men are going to work. We didn't imagine that the women were going to work. When we arrived at Auschwitz, our big question was, how soon will we see the men. We didn't know that they were going to be killed.

They lined us up—men on one side and women on the other side. We were inching always close to officers. As we were standing in line, my father was standing with two of my brothers, and my mother and my youngest brother were standing in one line. Pretty soon my father came from his line—he ran over to us—and he told my mother that he should take my mother's wedding ring, her diamond ring, that maybe he could get a slice of bread for it. He said surely they wouldn't take the bread away from him, or he might barter that for some food and bring it to us. Little did he know that within hours he would be dead, bread or no bread.

Dr. Josef Mengele—a horrible, horrible man—was standing at the front of the line with other officers. They had sticks in their hands, and they told us to go to the right or the left. To the right meant we were chosen to go to work, because we were young and strong. To the left, people were taken and gassed.

We kept asking the old prisoners, "When are we going to see our parents?" They said, "Don't worry about that. Go on, go on." Everything was hurry, hurry. They were trying to kill as many people as they could within a short period of time, because the Russians had started bombing all around us. I later found out that my parents and my brothers Artur and Arnold were killed that first day, May 22, 1944. Only 50 years later did I learn that my remaining brother, Tibor, did not die in Auschwitz, but was sent to a labor camp, Mauthausen, where he worked side-by-side with my cousin, Hersi, lifting heavy stones. The labor was too much for Tibor, and he died in December 1944. I am the only survivor from my immediate family.

Life in Auschwitz
First Days

When you went to Auschwitz, there were barracks (lagers or camps) by A, B, C. They sent a group of us young women and young mother—I mean not mothers with babies, but a mother with daughters old enough to work—to A Camp. To be chosen to work, you had to look young and healthy. My little brother was only 12 years old, and my mother was sort of chubby, so they wouldn't have her. I was with Aunt Magda, Uncle Louis's wife, and some other cousins. There were ten of us. We didn't work together, but we were in the same camp.

They gave me a piece of bread when I first arrived, and I put it under my straw mattress. When I woke up, the bread was gone. Somebody had stolen it. I had a cup I kept tied around my waist, and I slept on the cup too, but it was a little higher under the mattress, so I didn't lose it. When my bread was stolen the first night, I didn't have anything to eat. I said, "Where did I come to, to this wild world?" But God gave us strength. We still were young and the bread was stolen shortly after we arrived, so we managed somehow until the next time when we got bread.

Shortly after we were taken, was a holiday called Shavout,[1] a spring holiday. We were all sort of observant Jews, and one woman remembered the prayers. So we all stood up and repeated the prayers after her. We were just hoping that we wouldn't be caught doing this. And we weren't.

---

1   Shavuot occurs in late May or early June and commemorates the anniversary of the day God gave the Torah to the Jews.

Processed for Work in Birkenau

We stayed a few days in A Camp. Then they came to recruit women to work for factories in Germany that manufactured radios. In alphabetical order, an officer chose women up to last name initial "R" to work. I was among them. But I had an aunt, my mother's sister, with me. And she said, "You gonna leave me?" So when the officer turned around, I went back to be with her.

Then we were tattooed[2] and taken to Birkenau to work, which is the small camp at Auschwitz next to the crematorium. They put us in a sauna, and stripped off our clothes. Before the shower they shaved our heads and our privates. They had pharmacists who would douche the prisoners. Then with a rag they took disinfectant from a pail and put it on our heads and our bottoms. Officers would come in with dogs and guns and whips and just walk among the women, for no reason. They gave us clothing, In the beginning, we had just a gray cotton prisoner dress. I found my own shoes, but they wouldn't let me wear them. I had to walk in big men's shoes, size 42 European, which here is a women's size 11. At night, if we could, we washed our dress and hung it to dry and then slept just in panties and whatever we could find. There was no soap. We just had to use any water we had, and rub the cloth to take out the worst.

At the beginning we were commuting by foot from Auschwitz to Birkenau every day. We would walk from the A Camp to Birkenau every morning and every evening. They gave us white kerchiefs so they could identify us, and grey prisoner's vests. That's all we had, with the dress we got after the sauna. Later we sometimes got clothing from things new arrivals had brought. Clothing, if it fit, we put on. You couldn't have a long coat. If it was a long coat, you

---

2   Lola's number, recorded on her identity affidavit paper in 1948, was A–5887 (Figure 13). Auschwitz was the only complex in which prisoners were tattooed. The United States Holocaust Museum website, http://www.ushmm.org/wlc/en/article.php?ModuleId=10007056, and the website of Jewish Virtual Library, http://www.jewishvirtuallibrary.org/jsource/Holocaust/tattoos1.html, each contain excellent summaries of the history of the practice.

had to cut it off, because we would have gotten too warm in a long coat. Some women came with knitted panties to keep warm.

We commuted on foot from A Camp in Auschwitz to work in Birkenau for two or three weeks. Then they built barracks in Birkenau, and we moved there. After I moved to the dormitories in Birkenau, I found out that one of my professors was in the same barracks. One day she found out that I had a little more privileges, so I was able to rinse out my dress overnight and wear it clean the next morning. She asked if I would give her my clean dress and she would give me her lice-infested dress. So we went to the latrine and exchanged dresses.

About the second or third day after I came to Birkenau, I met a French Jewish inmate who was working outside on the garbage heap, and he said to me, "You see that chimney? That is the only way out of here." In the barrack, there were people from all over Europe—from France, from Italy, from Greece, and even a mother and two daughters from Algiers from North Africa. One French woman behind me spoke a little English and so did I, so I told her what the Frenchman said, that the only way out was through the chimney. When I came to the front of the barrack, an officer who overheard me stood there and slapped me on my face. I was glad that that was all he did to me—just one slap. But I remember it. He was an injured soldier from the front that came to volunteer and work in Auschwitz. He was from Vienna, and he was pretty mean. So we realized right away what went on. Plus, from the moment we got there, the transports never stopped coming.

Daily Routine

The food that was given to us was a piece of bread in the morning and a so-called "soup" at night. The soup consisted of potato peelings, with some pasternak, a root vegetable in it. If you use a little pasternak, it's ok, but if you use a lot it's bitter, so it wasn't tasty. And they threw bromide into the food, to make us not think clearly and be confused and not realize what was going on. It had other adverse health effects on us. We were given chemicals in the coffee and in the food, which meant we had no periods. Some people say, "That was from hunger." It could be. And the severe stress sometimes stops menstruation. And fear, might have had an effect. But everybody stopped menstruating—it was universal. That happened to everybody.

The guards would wake us up. We had to go to bed around nine o'clock at night. Then they woke us up at two or three for zählappell —counting off, standing in line. They had us call "zähl ab." That would last until it got light, from two in the morning until about six or seven. If a person stands still too long, the person tends to get faint. So we were pinching each other. One girl would pinch another girl's cheeks to make her look pink, to have red cheeks and stay upright. And mothers would slap their daughters' faces—there were quite a few mothers from Svalava. If the mothers were young and the daughters were able to work, then they left them together.

We got up, and when the zählappell ended, we stood in line to get a piece of bread—only one piece of bread a day, and it was chalky—and a cup of coffee, with chicory. We didn't drink that much. The coffee was awful. Then we went to work and worked all day. There was no lunch time as I recall, nothing. You just worked through until six o'clock. At six o'clock you got a bowl of the potato-peeling and pasternak soup.

Someone asked me what it was like in the camps when we weren't working. We got up so very early that by 9 o'clock in the evening, we went to sleep. We couldn't walk around. We just had to be in the barracks, in our bunk beds, right after dinner, which was the bowl of soup, which we ate sitting on our bunk beds. A newspaperman asked me, "What did you talk about when you weren't working?" I said, "We exchanged recipes. That kept us from feeling hungry." Recipes of what our mothers baked, and what meals she cooked.

The guards did take us every night after work to the sauna to take a shower. We only had one dress, and we would wash it whenever we had a little water, and we would hang it on a nail to dry overnight. When the camp was lice-infested, our entertainment after work was to get our dress off and kill the lice in the dress seams and in our hair with our fingernails. It was awful. There was a latrine. Sometimes, with somebody watching that the guard shouldn't come, somebody would have a little burner there, and they would be cooking whatever they had, whatever they found.

There were only two dormitories in Birkenau, and the rest of the barracks were for work. Later on they wanted to distinguish between the two barracks that were near the crematorium where we worked at Birkenau. They didn't have prisoner's clothes. So one barrack had navy blue polka-dotted dresses, and we had red polka-dotted dresses. If the dresses were long, they made us cut them short.

What work went on there? When they took the people into the crematorium, their suitcases were brought to prisoners in our part of the camp and emptied in different barracks. Others sorted out the contents. There were different girls and men who sorted things in the barracks. I was in a group of ten with some cousins and some girls from my hometown, Svalava. We were called the Träger Kommando. In the group with me, were my aunt, Magda Goldstein, three of my Goldstein cousins (Klara, Irene, and Manyi), three of my Oberländer cousins (Drezu, Bobi, and Olga), and my friends, the Bodek sisters (Elizabeth and Olga).

Elsewhere in the camp, my cousin Manya Berkovits worked a different work barrack. The three Birnbaum sisters worked in the same barrack. Two of the Birnbaum sisters worked sorting out the clothing that came from the crematorium. The third sister worked with pharmacists who found medicines in the things prisoners brought in, and sorted them out. My job was one of ten women carrying these bundles of sorted goods to the separate barracks, marching back and forth. One barrack was for medicines. One barrack was for clothing. One barrack was for blankets and sheets. And we carried them.

Many people had hidden jewelry, so a lot of jewelry was found in jars of jam, in the hems of the coats, in other places. Workers separated the gold jewelry that was found and gathered that. Once we were told that this big case of jewelry was full, and a truck was going to come and pick it up. My cousin, Bobi Oberländer, and I were selected to pick up the box filled with jewelry and put it in the back of the truck, and then go along when they took it to the warehouse. As we were riding in the back of the truck, the driver said, "Give me some jewelry and I will give you some bread and salami." I just reached into the box, and there were chains and watches and rings, and I grabbed some and handed them through a little window into the front of the truck. We took a big chance, on his part and on our part, because if we had been caught, we would have been killed instantly. So they had the jewelry, and we never heard from them again.

There was a sense of camaraderie at Auschwitz. If you found something—a piece of bread, a little sugar—before the officers would come by, you would put it under the table and put some sugar on the piece of bread and eat that. That was a treat. If we found some prunes, we would put them in a jar with water and make them swell so we could eat them. When we had some rice, a woman would have a little Sterno cooker in the latrine, which had been found among the belongings. Someone watched that an officer shouldn't come, and we would take turns and cook up a little something.

Music was playing every morning. They had a whole orchestra of musicians they found among the inmates. They played arias from operas and all kinds of compositions. There was a book and a movie made about this. It was called, "Playing For Time." There was a sign above the gates to Auschwitz: "Arbeit Macht Frei," which means that work will liberate you.

One thing that they made us do sometimes was they gave us pajamas and blankets and beach balls, and they put us in front of the road where the transports arrived. They made us play with the balls so that the people on the transport should see us and think they are coming to a resort. They also gave us postcards to write to some family left behind, so that the Germans can go and get them and bring the to the death camps, too. We couldn't keep the pajamas or the ball. They took them back to be used on another occasion.

One of the women prisoners was a ballerina from Athens, Greece. One time the guards gathered us in the sauna to see her dance ballet. They gave her a tutu, like a ballerina wears. And she was performing Ravel's Bolero. Every time I hear that music, my hair stands on end and I get a shudder—I can see her dancing there. Naturally, there were soldiers behind us, with guns. Piri, Elsa, and Bubi Birnbaum were in different barracks than I was. The sisters came into our barracks, because they knew somebody there, and they would sing in a low tone. I remember them singing a song about Niagara Falls. Shortly after they arrived, the sisters were already working, and some German officers found out they could sing, so they woke them up, and took them to their apartment, because they lived right near the camp. The officers also heard that they were good cooks, so they had them cook a dinner for the officers when they sang. These were officers who were not so bad, because they were at injured at the front and then were sent to work at Auschwitz.

> [Piri and Bubie were the main singers, and Piri's daughter amplified the experience in an email to Lola Taubman's cousin, Julie Ellis, in spring 2011:]
>
> "It all began one evening, when the girls in the Block in Auschwitz were very sad. My mother wanted to cheer them up a little, so she and her sister began to sing together. A Nazi officer heard them. He liked their singing, and took them from that day on to sing before the Nazi soldiers. They sang almost every night in front of the Nazi soldiers. My mother told me how difficult it was to sing with her head shaved, only a few days after she had seen her parents for the last time. My mother told me that the famous musician, Smuel Gogol, who played the harmonica, accompanied them."

Witness to Evil

At Birkenau, when we were commuting, marching from one Auschwitz camp to the other, we saw these trucks go by with people on them. People who were interned, and couldn't walk and they were being taken on trucks to the crematorium. We would just see them go in that building and never come out. We couldn't say anything.

You knew that something happened to these people. You would never see them come out. They were only taken in these buildings. And I saw some of the German officers throw the gas in these little windows with iron bars, and then slam the windows shut. When we arrived, they were running short of Zyklon, so they threw in a little bit, just enough to stun the people. You couldn't hear screaming, because the walls were so thick. And the windows were closed. Then they would take the bare bodies, put them in the trucks that lifted up dumped them in a pile and burned them, half alive.

I can tell you that no nation in the history of the world acted in the barbaric way the Germans did. They were cruel to the worst degree. By the time we arrived, they didn't have enough gas to kill people completely, so when they were half-alive they put them on trucks, and across the camp where I was—you know how the trucks lift up (miming truck bed lifting at an angle) and dump the contents. And they were burned half-alive. Every time I go near a restaurant that broils or barbecues meat, I can still smell that odor. It is a similar smell to the way the corpses were burned.

There was a girl that was our next-door neighbor—she was in camp with me—and somebody told her that they saw her father being brought into Birkenau to be gassed. There was nothing that she could do to stop her father from being killed. She could see him being taken into this building.

The big bundles of possessions continued to come to our camp, and the smoke just went on. Grandmothers on these trucks carried little step stools for their grandchildren. They carried balls. We saw babies fall off from trucks. Then the next truck would come and run over the baby. And dolls fell off. Dolls and toys were strewn all over the road.

A young schoolgirl once asked, "Did you ever see Adolf Hitler?" No. He wouldn't come near the camp. That was too dangerous for him to do. He was afraid there might be an uprising, killings. Dr. Mengele was in my camp quite often. There was a girl that I knew, and she found out that a friend of hers was in the camp next to us—we were separated by an electrical fence. She threw a package across the fence, and she was caught while Mengele was in her camp. Every once in a while, he came to see how efficiently the organization was working. And he ordered that the girl be beaten. Two or three officers took turns beating her. When she passed out, they would pour a pitcher of water on her and continue beating her. That girl came back after the war with a murmur in her heart, and she died at a young age. There were beatings all the time. Some mean guards were drunk most of the time. I don't know if the mean guards drank to forget what they had seen, or that was just their habit.

I met a young man after the war in one of the camps. He had been born in Sweden, and was on a visit to Germany when they grabbed him and put him in Auschwitz, and he was used in some of Dr. Mengele's experiments. He eventually got a disease from these experiments, and he was on crutches. Small German children used to tease him by calling, "Cripple, cripple." He got so mad that he would take the crutch and beat the kids up. No other country would have him because he had this disease. He couldn't come to the United States. He couldn't go anywhere. We left Germany, and I don't know what happened to him.

I had identical twin cousins from Izvor where my father was born. There were lots of twins in our family. Their family lived next door to my grandmother in that little village, Izvor, and when we visited her we also visited that family, who had six children, I remember my aunt standing over the stove and cooking a lot of soup. These twins were in our camp. One twin was used by Mengele for experiments. They put him in a laboratory and they performed experiments on him They put a metal capsule that had gas in it inside his bones, and they lit a match to it. They wanted to see what the effect to the bone was from the heat produced by the metal. He survived, but as a result, he got tuberculosis of the bones, and he died in Israel at a young age. He only lived to be about forty-two. He was married, but was never able to have a child. The other twin worked in the crematorium as a Sonderkommando, putting the dead bodies into the oven.[3] The Sonderkommandos were tattooed on their foreheads, and worked for only six months. After six months, they were shot, and a new group was selected. I recognized a doctor who was a dermatologist. They put him to work there to remove gold fillings and gold crowns from the bodies.

Just before the end, before we were evacuated, there was an uprising in the crematorium. Somebody smuggled guns to the workers. When the workers got the guns, they decided on the uprising. There was such tension. The guards made sure we didn't leave the barracks, so we wouldn't see what was going on, but there were cracks in the wooden walls of the barracks, and we were able to see. When the uprising took place, they just shot them all. It was at the end already, just before we left Auschwitz. My cousin who was a Sonderkommando perished in the uprising.

Later, in Florida, a schoolgirl asked me, "How do you feel about the Germans now. Do you have a lot of hatred for them?" You can never forget. It was just too horrific. So I don't forgive too easily. How can you forgive? Would any of you forgive if it had been done to you what was done to my family?

One schoolboy asked if we had any sympathetic guards. Some of them were a little easier than other ones. I remember one guard toward the end of the war that was fairly decent. He had a secretary that was from Slovakia, who was a very smart girl. She got sick. She had pneumonia just before we left. He provided a horse and wagon to put her on the wagon so she shouldn't have to march. After the war, there was a trial, and people came and spoke on his behalf, and he was let free.

A schoolgirl asked if I knew how many of the officers were actually sentenced and punished. I don't know exactly, but very, very few. You know, some bigwigs even committed suicide, like Goebbels and Goering, and Hitler himself. A schoolboy said he had heard that a lot of officers left Germany and went to other

---

3   The Sonderkommandos were Jewish prisoners forced to dispose of the bodies of the gas chamber victims by loading them into the ovens of the crematorium.

countries. He knew some had gone to South America, and he wanted to know if a lot of them were found. So far, they only found Eichmann. And another one of them was deported to Italy—he was on trial many years later when he was almost 80 years old, and he said, "I was just following orders." Following orders! He didn't have to be brutal when following orders. I don't know if you are aware of it, but the Vatican helped many of the Nazis. They were given papers, and first they went to Spain and Portugal, and eventually to Argentina and Brazil. They escaped right after the war. I was taken from camp to camp in Germany. For four years I waited for the Czech quota to come to the United States. By then these Nazis had a good life after perpetrating all those atrocities on us.

Later on we questioned how could God do this to us. We weren't criminals. We didn't harm anybody. For the simple reason that we were born Jews, we had to be punished so severely. After one talk in a school in Florida, a boy said he knew Hitler's soldiers had to obey him because they were in the military, and he asked if I blamed them that they had to kill all those people because they were given orders. I said the camps couldn't have been done without the cooperation of the entire nation. They could have had an uprising, like they do in other countries. These were professors, doctors, and engineers. They were such a cultured people, they should have known better. You know why they were escaping after the war? They were too cowardly to face up to their deeds and be judged.

End of War Turmoil
Final Death Marches

We did all this work until, toward the beginning of 1945, we left Auschwitz. We were there from the beginning of May 1944 until January 18, 1945. January 18 was only five days before the Russians marched in. We had to burn all the heaps of blankets, eyeglasses, and clothing, and records. They didn't want anything left, so that they could be held accountable for it. We went on a death march from Birkenau. It was January. It was snowing. We wore just a short jacket and a dress of material that they use for ropes [hemp], and I had unlined size 42 men's shoes. When we came to the edge of Auschwitz, there were anti-aircraft guns pointing at the sky. We were very frightened, because we didn't know what was going to happen. I was so scared that they would point those guns at us. We marched on foot from Poland to the German border. I was together with my Aunt Manci Oberländer (my mother's youngest sister), and she held my piece of bread, and when I asked if she would give me a piece, she said, "No, I'm saving it. When you pass out, I'll give it to you then. Just eat snow." We didn't know it was a "death march." We found out. If you couldn't walk well, you would be beaten because you weren't going fast enough. If you couldn't walk faster, they would shoot you.

Then, once again, they put us on boxcars. This time, the boxcars were open. The snow fell right on us. We went through towns where the heaviest bombings of the war were happening—to Dessau, and Magdeburg, and Dresden. Finally we came into Berlin. That was the worst bombing we had ever seen. In Berlin, all the Allies were bombing at the same time—the Russians, the French, the English, and the Americans. Half of the train was demolished, and the women in that half died. I was lucky to be in the half that was not damaged. They had to fix the railroad, because the rails were standing up. The officers went into a bunker to try to save their lives, and they were safe. We had to stay put. We had no food—I don't know how we survived.

Ravensbrück

After a few days, they fixed the tracks and attached an engine, and we were shipped on. We went to a camp called Ravensbrück.[4] It was a bad camp. It started out for women political prisoners. Not Jews. We arrived at Ravensbrück in the middle of the night. The railroad arrived in a wooded area with pine trees on either

4   Ravensbrück, the largest German concentration camp for women, was located 90 km north of Berlin near the village of Ravensbrück. (United States Holocaust Memorial Museum Holocaust Encyclopedia website.)

side, just standing. I was so scared when we arrived, I said, "Oh my God, again—electrical fences." They unloaded us and put us in barracks. It was a horrible camp. There were corpses all over. There were bunk beds stacked three high. There was typhoid fever and dysentery. I found out that a classmate of mine and her mother were in the camp. We went to see them. When we got to their barrack, they were on the upper bunk, and they couldn't recognize us. They were just skeletons. They were delirious and near death. They never made it out of there.

I shared a narrow bunk bed with a woman, and I didn't know she was pregnant. She was delivering the baby that night. There were no scissors. Everybody said, "do you have a knife, do you have a knife?" Nobody had anything. They tore the umbilical cord, and they threw the baby away to save the woman. A student asked me later if the guards would have killed the mother who had the baby, if they had found it. I replied that, yes, they would have killed her. They would have been sorry they didn't kill her when she arrived, because usually if somebody was pregnant, they were taken along with the older people to be killed.

We had to stand in line to get our one meal a day, some concoction of soup. One day, after I made my way to the kettle, I took off a can I had saved and had on a string around my waist, and when I got my soup I turned around, and a Ukrainian inmate intentionally knocked it out of my hands. That is what anti-Semitism was, everywhere, everywhere. The women guards were so ruthless, and the soldiers. Guns and dogs everywhere.

Finally I got sick too, I got dysentery. We were given ten minutes to go to the latrine. While I was there, I passed out. I heard the whistle blowing to signal that the ten minutes were up. But I couldn't get up. I heard the girls shouting, "Hurry up because there is a guard coming." I staggered out of the latrine, and sure enough, a soldier was pointing a gun at me. For some reason, he didn't shoot me, and I got back. It was meant for me to live.

Malchow

We were in Ravensbrück about two weeks, and they decided to move us out. They put us in open boxcars and took us to another camp. We were on that train for at least two days, because we had to stop every time they needed the rails. Malchow was in the state of Mecklenburg, not far from the North Sea, near Lübeck.[5] I had socks when we were taken in open cars from Ravensbrück to Malchow. My feet were so cold I took the socks off. There was sort of a rod and I put them there to dry. The wind blew them away so I had no more socks. I got frostbite. I have two toes that are frostbitten. They didn't give me trouble until I was older. Now they swell up and I have to see what shoes I can wear.

We didn't do any work in Malchow. It was a holding camp, a German army camp. There were little buildings. We had rooms. Some rooms were bigger and some rooms were smaller. I was in one room with twenty-eight girls, most of whom had typhoid fever or dysentery. Women were dying daily. I was the only one that didn't get sick. Again we only got one soup a day and a piece of bread. There was a woman from Munkacs, and she was working in the kitchen, and her mother was ashamed of her because she wouldn't help us.

I knew everybody that was in my room (my Aunt Manci Oberländer was there), and we tried to help each other. There was some sort of water fountain where we washed our hands and face, and sometimes we would wash our dress. First we would take the lice out. All the seams had lice in them. We would stand and kill the lice, and then wash and hang the dress on a nail on the wall to dry overnight. I don't know what I slept in, panties I guess. We just kept each other warm because it was so crowded. When we slept, when one turned, everybody else turned. They woke us up at two or three in the morning just to stand in line so they could count us.

---

5   Malchow was one of the largest of the over 40 subcamps of Ravensbrück, according to the website of the United States Holocaust Memorial Museum, Washington, D.C. Today it is a small site on the map near "Mecklenberg" to the east of Lübeck.

God forbid we could have escaped—I don't know how. They did this in Auschwitz and all the camps.

Leipzig-Schönefeld

After a few weeks in Malchow, they decided to move us out again. They came and selected people to work in an ammunition factory in Leipzig. So, again, we were on a train. Half of my relatives went to another camp. Elizabeth Wees and Olga and my cousins and me were chosen to work in Leipzig-Schönefeld.[6] They shipped us from Malchow to Leipzig in East Germany, to the suburb of Schönefeld, where there was an ammunition factory. When we finally arrived at Leipzig, there was a three-story dormitory. At that time, they didn't know who was Jewish and who was not, so they put us all in that building. But within a day, some of the non-Jews reported us who were Jewish. Then the non-Jews insisted that we should leave. So they took us out of the dormitory and put us in some wooden barracks.

We had to work. They put me right away in the night shift at the ammunition factory. The factory was right next door to the dormitory. The factory had no sign outside. You couldn't tell what went on there. Deceiving, deceiving all the time. There were nightly bombings, so every time they bombed, they would send us into the bunker under the factory. One day a bomb hit the brick dormitory, and the non-Jewish women perished. We were saved in the wooden barracks. Apparently whoever bombed—the Russians or the Americans—knew that the Jewish inmates were in the wooden barracks. They had enough Intelligence. As a matter of fact, when we met some liberated American prisoners of war, they said every time the soup was bad, they would send a message and the bombers would come. Every time the bombers came, it was such a pressure on our ears, some women had punctured eardrums and lost their hearing. I was lucky it didn't happen to me.

---

6   The ammunition factory at Leipzig-Schönefeld was part of the Hugo Schneider AG (HASAG) sites producing ammunition for the Nazis. (A Wikipedia article covers the history of the firm.)

My job was with cannon shells. The shells were about 12 inches long. And you had to put one into a machine, and the machine stretched it to a longer size. I had a little "supervisor," and she was Ukrainian, and she told me that if I didn't want to be beaten up, I had better learn how to sabotage. The sabotage meant that when a cannon shell was put into the machine, I shouldn't push the button at a certain time, but wait, and when I pushed it at the wrong time, it would smash the cannon shell. There were two wagons. One was for the rejects and one was for the good cannon shells. A German officer came and asked me how come there were so many rejects. And I said, "I don't know. There is something wrong with the machine." Anyhow, I wasn't punished, but they found out about the Ukrainian girl—that she said some wrong things—and they punished her. Every other week they shaved her head, but she didn't care. Every time the Russian bombers would come, she would run out and wave the kerchief to them.

Marching Around Leipzig

After a few weeks, they finally bombed the factory and flattened it while we were in the bunker, and there was nothing left for us to do there. We were surrounded by Allied forces, but the Germans were so mean, they wouldn't give us a chance to be liberated. They wouldn't let us free. After the bombing was finished, they decided to evacuate us.[7] We went on another death march around Leipzig. We went around and around. We were wandering like a cat and dog. We were in every village two or three times. When we went through the villages, the people looked out and quickly shuttered their windows. They didn't want to see us.

So we were marching. The mother of a friend was dying and they were just dragging her, and finally, they were left behind. The mother died on the way, and they buried her alongside the road. It was coming towards the end of the war and the Germans were

---

7   According to the United States Holocaust Museum online Holocaust Encyclopedia, on March 28, 1945, the Leipzig-Schönefeld camp housed 4,765 female prisoners. In early April 1945, "the SS evacuated many of the inmates to prevent them from falling into Allied hands."

retreating. We saw damaged personnel carriers and tanks. They made us lie in the ditch along the road, so that they could have the roads free for them. We were so tired that we would fall asleep in the ditch. Once, all of a sudden, a tank came and mowed down some of the women. One woman—one of the Sternbach girls that lived not far from where we lived in Svalava—had her leg crushed. My cousin Irene was very good friends with her. Her name was Lily. She was lucky, because she had a high boot, and it kept her leg together. I happened to have a raw potato and a spoon. I scraped the potato and gave the bits to her in her mouth, that she shouldn't faint. You can imagine, for us to see that.

Along the march, again they needed the roads, and they put us in a soccer field. One of the horses that was pulling a wagon with supplies for the Germans died, so they butchered the horse, and they gave us the horsemeat. I wouldn't eat it, but we were together with some gypsies—women—and they didn't mind eating the horsemeat. So I traded them. There was a sack of rice that was broken open, so a gypsy woman gave me rice, and I gave her the horsemeat. Then I gathered some grass, and I had an empty can, and I put in the grass and the rice and a little water. Some women gathered some twigs, and we made a fire. I was ready to cook the little rice; then the whistle blew—to march on, and the rice was never cooked.

One day they put us in a barn, because again they needed the roads. Two of the boards in the barn were broken, and I looked out and I saw that there was a girl digging in a mound where there were potatoes. So I thought, I'll run out, and I will get a potato too. When I went there, they started yelling, "Look out, because a guard is coming." I turned around, and he shot the girl next to me. She was from Holland. It could have been me. So I believe that if it is meant for some person to live, the person is going to live, no matter what.

We marched for two weeks. Then we saw demolished military equipment. Little by little the guards left us. I heard the story—I didn't see it myself—that one guard asked if he could have the camp uniform, so that he could escape. The Germans guards didn't actually have to worry, because if they stopped at any farm, the farmers would have helped them. The farmers were scared of the Russians—not so much of the Americans, and not of the French or the English—they were only scared of the Russians, because they had a bad reputation; they would force themselves on women.

The guards put us into an abandoned school. They just had straw in the gymnasium, and we slept there. There were no doctors to take care of our wounds. There was no food. I don't know how we survived. Finally we decided we were not going to stay in that camp, and we found an empty German house, and we stayed there.

Finally, the officers that were guarding us all left, and what did we see? A tank arrived, and there were Americans and Russians on it. They were celebrating, sort of meeting each other, and fighting on. They were jumping on each other's tanks, singing and flag-waving. They had a loud radio playing—the first radio I heard was at liberation when the Russians and the Americans met—and I heard the American radio saying that President Roosevelt died. This was toward the end of April.

Life as a Displaced Person

On the Road

The war wasn't over for a few more days, so there was nobody to take care of us. They were busy fighting on until May 5th or 6th. We were left just without anybody. The Americans didn't have time to take care of us. The Germans refused. Some of those who met the Americans earlier, got food. They got chocolate and they got sardines, and they ate too fast and got sick and died. We had no food. We were just abandoned.

We were some cousins together and some friends—there were about four girls. People were injured; they had sores. There was not a doctor to take care of wounds, no medicine or anything. We had nothing to cover ourselves, no food. One girl from our hometown, she had a good voice, and she tried to sing. People weren't very anxious to give us food. We were in a village, and we were just wandering around. All the farms had fences and gates. If we walked to a German farm, they wouldn't give us any food. The German farmers were afraid that we were Russians, and we were going to rape them and take everything away, which the Russians did. Anything that was not nailed down, they took. Two girls—one from my class and one from my hometown—they were raped, and then they were shot. It's not enough to rape, but they killed them.

So when we were on our own, we were hiding on a farm in a hayloft, and we tried to be so quiet, because the Russians were marching through, and we didn't know what they were going to do to us. We slept there. We also slept in bombed-out houses in the basements. I remember that one of the Sternbach girls was singing there, and we also heard birds singing for the first time in a year, because, in Auschwitz, they were too scared of the smoke.

We met some Yugoslav prisoners of war—there were some good ones and some bad ones. These Yugoslavs said "Come with us, we'll get you food." They didn't care; they went to a farm and knocked the gate down and went in. The Yugoslavs gave us some food. Then they confiscated some bicycles and gave them to us. I never knew how to ride a bicycle. My father had two brothers that worked for us, and they used bicycles to collect the money that people owed. One of them said he was going to teach me how to ride, so I got on the bicycle and said, "What do you do when a car comes." "Just keep pumping." And I fell, and I never learned. Now, when I said I didn't know how to ride, my cousin said, "Don't give me that. Don't worry about it. Just get on that bicycle and pedal." I don't know where I got the courage or the strength to do it, but I pedaled for about two or three kilometers. Then the Russians came and took the bicycles away, and loaded them on their wagon to ship them to Russia.

We heard there was a bombed-out food depot, so we were running to find it. But the Germans had burned it. There were cans that were exploded, and some sugar that had melted. When I tried to eat some of the sugar, I chipped my tooth because there was gravel in it. Some of the Russians had stayed back, and they tried to entice us to come into their camp so that they could take us with them back to Russia. We were reluctant, but I had a toothache, and they had a little medical tent, so I decided to go there. A Russian woman dentist came. She had her hair shaved off, just a beret on. (You know, the doctors and the dentists shaved their heads, because they didn't want to be bothered with hairdos—they just wore a beret.) Instead of drilling and filling that tooth, this dentist pulled the nerve out of two teeth. They turned black, so I arrived in the United States with two black teeth. Later in Detroit, instead of covering them with crowns, they pulled them—healthy teeth that didn't have any nerve.

Prague

One day, we heard that a Czech officer from the Overseas Army was coming. He was looking for his relatives. He couldn't find any, but he said, "Don't worry, I'll take care of you." So he went back to Czechoslovakia, and he sent a bus to take all the Czech citizens to Prague. Well, there were all kinds of people there—from Poland, from Hungary, from Romania, and everybody jumped on the bus. In Auschwitz, somebody had found my father's jacket. In it was his picture, so I kept this picture with me all this time. I had hung onto that picture throughout. At the last minute, when the bus came to take us back to Czechoslovakia, we were all in such a hurry that I left the little pillow and the picture I hid under it. When the bus came to take us, I was in such a hurry that I left the picture there.

So we came to Prague, the capitol of Czechoslovakia. That's when I found my uncles. When we arrived at Prague, we came to a square, and there were some men from slave labor waiting there, welcoming every bus that came and looking for relatives. They told me that two of my father's brothers survived. None of my own family survived. I thought then that all my brothers went with my father to the crematorium in Auschwitz. But fifty years later, a cousin of mine told me that one brother was in camp with him. My father comes from a family of eleven. Three were already in the United States. Of the others, only the two uncles I found in Prague survived. My mother was one of nine, and the only aunt I had left, she died at age 52 after the war of brain cancer.

The two uncles I found in Prague, both had joined the Army of the Czech government in exile. The government, from London, formed an army with Russia, Ukraine, and Poland. But Stalin had his plans, so he ordered the Czech Army not to go to Carpathia, where I was from, but to go to Bohemia in the Czech Republic, because he was going to occupy that part—Bohemia, Silesia, Moravia, Slovakia, and Carpathia. The uncles ended up in Siberia. Uncle Zigmund was in a hospital in Siberia, and when they bombed it, and it was on fire, he jumped out of the second story; and he fell in the snow, and he went to a farmer, and that's how he survived. My Uncle Louis was in Siberia in a camp, and he had typhoid fever, and he had such high fever that he was delirious. So he went out in the snow barefooted, and he said that his mother was waiting for him at the gate—which wasn't so. But he froze his toes. And without anesthetic, they operated and they amputated all his toes.

Now, both these uncles were in Prague, where they met up in the Czech Legion. Uncle Zigmund was given a business by the government, and an apartment in Teplitz-Shanov. He married a younger woman and had two children. Uncle Louis, as an officer in the Czech army, was given an apartment in Prague.

[A second excerpt from the memoir of Lola's uncle, Louis Goldstein, provides a summary of his astonishing experiences from 1942 to his arrival in Prague in May 1945:]

"In September of 1942, I had to report to a slave labor camp in Kisvárda. From there we were transferred to the Russian front in the area of Osztrogoszk and Voronezh. In December 1942, we were captured by the Russians and became prisoners of war. At this point, I completely lost contact with my wife and family. I had absolutely no knowledge about them and did not hear of them until the end of the war.... I was one of 15,000 POWs. From Osztrogoszk, we were transported ... to a POW camp in Morshansk.... We arrived ... on January 20, 1943. After extremely harsh conditions and a typhoid epidemic, only about 500 prisoners remained alive.... I was ... hospitalized, with frostbite, and my toes had to be amputated.... After recuperating from my injuries, I managed to work for a few months for a Russian Jewish officer, serving as his interpreter.... In the spring of 1944, several prisoners, citizens of Czechoslovakia, were allowed to join the Czechoslovak Legion, under the direction of General Svoboda. Despite many difficulties, I also managed to join this outfit, the so-called Zahranični Armada. After fighting the Germans from Poland to Slovakia to Moravia to Bohemia, the Legion finally reached Prague on May 5, 1945."

My Aunt Magda was with us, so she and Uncle Louis were reunited. They had married in 1942, but were separated after six weeks, when Uncle Louis was taken for slave labor. They didn't see each other until this time in Prague in 1945.

I also met the Birnbaum sisters again in Prague, and we were liberated together. When I came there, I was so weak—I only weighed 90 pounds—and I could barely step up into the streetcar. A Catholic organization named Caritas, which is "Charity," took us to a monastery run by nuns. The first good meal that we had was in Prague, when the nuns cooked soup and gave us bread. Then we got some United Nations clothes and shoes, because I was still in the size 42 men's shoes that I left in from Auschwitz.

Then, for a while, my cousins Manyi and Hersi, who had also come to Prague, lived with Uncle Zigmund, and I lived with Uncle Louis and Aunt Magda. Anybody that survived from the family and friends, all came to Uncle Louis and Aunt Magda's apartment. Food was hard to get in Prague, so the only meat we had was rabbit. Another cousin by marriage would bring rabbits; so we shared the cooked rabbit. The apartment building was in an "O" shape with a courtyard in the middle, and when you looked out, everybody had a rabbit hanging in the window. My Aunt Magda would cook, and everybody ate and had a cup of coffee. We didn't have a real coffee—it was chicory. The real home cooking was when my aunt cooked in Prague. We slept on the floor. Even this teacher—Opman—whose brother I went to school with in Munkacs, she slept on the floor there.

Bubi and Piri Birnbaum (and their brother, because he was a student), invited us on an outing to land near Prague, which is very nice farmland. Survivors of schools were sent there. We were there, and people brought whatever they had. We took the train; and they waited for us in a decorated horse and buggy, and we came there. We stayed in a big house. We helped dig potatoes. We helped cook. We got to pick blueberries. It felt very good. We were picking blueberries and making blueberry pie. But we didn't dare go in the villages. We heard that the Russians had some Czech agents working to spread communism, and they were trying to convince people to come with them. They said the farmers would be better off because they would have farm equipment that they could share.

Back to Germany
Hidden Journey

By the time we got back to Prague, things got worse. In 1946, Hungary started taking over Czechoslovakia, and we found out that the communists were more and more active. So we decided we were not going to stay in Prague. I got a call from Teplitz where my other uncle and cousins were, and they said, "We're going back to Germany. If you want to join us, board the train immediately." And I did. I had a suitcase and the handle broke on it; I didn't know what to do. Then I found out that in As, the town on the Czech-German border, there was a family, the Hechts, from our hometown, that survived, and they were living there. So I thought maybe they can help me. I tried to go to their house, and somebody said, "Watch out, somebody's following you." Again, communists wanted to stop people from leaving. They wanted them to stay in the country and join the communists and live in the communist regime. The Hechts were hiding me in a barn; then they got me a backpack, and I was able to try and cross the border.

We crossed the border illegally during the night. There was an organization of former Polish partisans who tried to get us across the border into Germany. They were called the bricha.[8] When we

---

8   The United States Memorial Holocaust Museum website says,

came to the border, we had to wait for a Czech border guard who was willing to be bribed. The first night we didn't make it, and they said that everybody that had a baby or a child should watch that they shouldn't cry. There were Russian Jewish children, and that was the first time I saw a child after the war. The women with children put Band Aids on the infants' mouths so they shouldn't cry and be detected, because if you had been, you would have been shot at the border.

Trying to Leave Germany for the USA

Finally we were successful, and we came into Germany again. We were met by Israeli soldiers, who welcomed us. We came to Munich, and from Munich they sent us to a displaced person's camp in Gabbersee,[9] Bavaria. I was there for a while. I met an American woman UN officer, and because I knew a little English, I worked with her. I worked registering people so they could apply to go to the United States. We stayed in Gabbersee for a while. I didn't have a towel, so I knew a woman who was married to a Jew, and they took her husband away to Auschwitz. They didn't kill her, so now she was the cook there. I asked this woman if I could have a towel for a pack of cigarettes; I got a towel and I kept it until I came to the US.

Then we were sent to another camp, in Bavaria, along a lake called Chiemsee. On that lake, on an island, was a castle of Ludwig the Second—a famous castle and people came to see. The nearby town was called Prien (-am-Chiemsee). We didn't know then, but later on we found out that Josef Eichmann—the notorious man who devised all of the methods of how to transfer people to Auschwitz and other camps—he was hiding in that village. Finally he left there and went to Argentina.

Manyi and Hersi, their cousins, and their sister, and a lot of

---

"Bricha was the organized illegal immigration movement of Jews from Eastern Europe across the occupied zones and into Israel."

9   Gabbersee was a DP camp, and a borough of Wasserburg am Inn, in Bavaria in the American zone of occupation. It was originally a military camp, and it was a first stop after getting back to Germany.

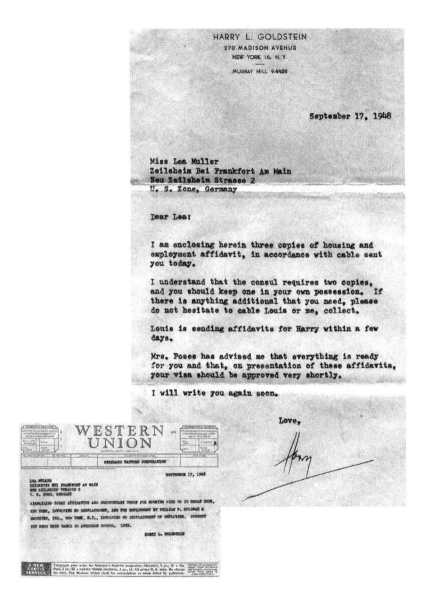

Figure 11

Letter and telegram from Lola's cousin, Harry L. Goldstein, to her as
Lea Müller, enclosing copies of the document attesting to
housing and employment, crucial to her successful
emigration in February 1949 from Germany to the United States.

Sternbachs were in Gabbersee. No relatives from my mother's family were with us at this point, because they were earlier chosen (in Auschwitz) to work for the Philips Company in Germany. The cousins who worked for Philips, a sister and brother, were liberated early, taken to Sweden. Bobi had one child in Sweden. They stayed there for a while. Then they decided to go to Israel, so the sister tried on one ship, and the brother tried on Exodus. Those on Exodus were already in Tel Aviv, when they returned them to Germany. They tried again on a different ship, and were taken to Cyprus.

After a while, those of us in Gabersee registered to go to the United States. There were a group of ten of us. We applied right away. Aunt Magda and Uncle Louis tried to help us get proper paperwork, but they were not successful. (A copy of a hand-written letter in English from them in Brooklyn shows their concern:)

Louis Goldstein
1381 – E. 23 Str.
Brooklyn N.Y.

Brooklyn November 6. 1946

Dear Loli, Manyi and Hersi

We received your letter of October 25th and you can imagine how happy we were to read some news. Unfortunately you are still not writing us about those things what we would wish mostly to know. Why are you not writing exactly if we have to make out a new affidavit or have you some possibility Loli with your affidavit sent by my uncle. If not why is it not good. I wrote you last week a letter also about those things, and you must those informations repeat in every letter because some of them are not arriving and so we miss the most important ones.

We really are shocked that you couldn't get over here till now, but please you must hope still and you will see everything will be all right.

Don't do any registration for Brasilie [Brazil]. It has no sense and it would [be] much more complicated to come over here from there as from Germany. So you must be patient a little it will go. I know it is hard for you there but unfortunately nothing goes so smoothly as we would wish.

We will try to send you a package this week. I hope you will get it in a short time.

We received from Budapest some letters. They are writing about receiving your New Years cards. They thank you for it and asking me to some to send you their best regards because from there is a very bad postal connection with Germany.

I hope you are healthy. Answer at once and write <u>exactly</u> what would be now the best to do for you. If you need a new affidavit with what dates. I hope it won't pass a long time and we will be able to see each other again.

Much love and many kisses to you all from Magda

[addition - different handwriting:]

My dear Loli, Hersi and Manyi !

We received your letter, write us more often and exactly what is to do in your interest. Sunday I spoke with Berkovics Oli, they received your letter too. I spoke with Berkowics Harry, he promised to make out a new affidavit for Hersi and Manyi. Dear Loli, if the affidavit from uncle Maurice Blaufeld isn't good, write at once, and we make out a new one. Write at once to us. Don't register to Brasilie. Learn all of you English, it is very important, if you have occasions to learn some trade, so do it, it is very important too. Enclosed one dollar.

Many regards from Louis.

It didn't take long, and we were called to the Consulate in Munich. We were there, and we were shivering, wondering was it going to be all right. The Consul comes out, and he says we cannot go to the United States now because we had left Germany, and only those who never left Germany have privileges. We had gone back to Prague for a while. We were punished for that, because those that had never left Germany had preference.

It was a big shock, but I worked with this very pleasant officer — a woman from Wisconsin. She said, "I will take care of you." First she was going to take us to villages and get us different names. And then we decided not to do it. We were put on a truck—there was a group of 10 people. And we went to Stuttgart, and they couldn't accept us there. The camp was too full, so we only stayed a few days. When we got to the Consulate in Stuttgart, we found they had sent out a list of the rejects to all the Consulates, so when we came to Stuttgart, they found our rejected names, so we couldn't apply.

Then they shipped those that were rejected—the group from Gabbersee—to Zeilsheim, a big camp near Frankfurt, and I got involved there too. We went there, but we didn't do anything yet, we were waiting. While I was in Zeilsheim I heard from a sort of boyfriend I had, who had gone to Bratislava to do some business when I left for Germany with Manyi and Hersi. Now he sent a man to take me back across the border to Czechoslovakia. When I came to the border, there was shooting and I never made it. And he got married to somebody. They went to Israel, and she didn't like it. She said if he doesn't take her back to Czechoslovakia, she is going to commit suicide. And they did go back to Czechoslovakia and settled there. I never heard from him, but I heard about him from an Israeli friend. It's bashert—it's meant to be.

DP Camps and Work

I worked in Zeilsheim for the Americans from the middle of 1946 to 1949.[10] In 1947, an Israeli officer came to Zeilsheim looking

---

10   Lola evidently learned to type in English doing the office work for the Americans in Gabbersee and Zeilsheim. Certainly, her English grew stronger.

Figure 12

Lola
Goldstein
and friends
in Zeilsheim
DP Camp,
1947.
Lola is 4th
from the right.
Aggi
Birnbaum
is 2nd from
the right,
and Manya
Berkovits
is at the
far left
of the row.

for somebody who spoke Hebrew to work in the Israeli Consulate in Frankfurt. So I worked part-time in the camp and part-time in Frankfurt.

The Israeli Consulate office was in the only temple in Frankfurt that was not bombed. The temple was beautiful. It was a Reform temple. They had an organ. It was on Friedrichstrasse that ended in a few blocks at the IG Farben building where Eisenhower had his headquarters. The rabbi's place was two stories. One story was HIAS [Hebrew Immigrant Aid Society]. One story was the Jewish Agency [For Palestine],[11] and they had several dormitories. This part of the temple was the rabbi's private space. There was one big room with several beds, and we slept there. During this time, we shared rooms with several other girls. We had food. Before the war, they had yeshiva bochurs[12] living and studying there.

I helped process papers for the people who were emigrating to the United States. I learned to type in Hebrew. I had never typed before. It was a very nice thing. The man I worked for was under the Consul, and he was very nice to me. He was from Germany, and he used to play the clarinet. The Consul was a woman, Rachel Adiv, and I befriended her. I visited her later in Israel. Her husband was an officer with the Israeli Haganah. She had a boyfriend in the meantime—the man I worked for—and he travelled all over, and they were going to buy guns and boats in Germany for the Aliyah Bet. So one time, he handed me his briefcase and said, "Put those things away." They had guns in there. I was so scared. What if they're loaded? I'm going to mishandle it and get shot.

I was helping people go to Israel, even though I didn't want to go to Israel myself because I was afraid of shooting. I didn't want to hear another gun. The Israelis didn't mind, because I said I was too scared to go because I didn't want to get another shooting. The war was going on in Israel. The British were not that great because every time an illegal boat came, they put it to Cyprus. And they

11   When the Jewish Agency for Palestine shut down in August 1948, they provided two letters of recommendation for Lola, as Lea. (Figure 17)

12   Yeshive bochurs were yeshiva boys.

Figure 13

Top: Lola Goldstein, Frankfurt in 1946.
Bottom: Lola with Rachel Adiv, with whom Lola worked in Frankfurt
from 1947 to 1948. Photo taken in Haifa in 1968.

even sunk two big ships with Jews on them, and they all drowned. We were hearing how people were surrounded in Jerusalem, and they couldn't get out. They couldn't get food. They couldn't get water. We were so upset, and we listened to the radio all the time.

But many people were ready to go, and they had to have papers. At the beginning, they just made arrangements. Some of them went on their own. Others didn't want to go on their own. They either went by legal Aliyah Aleph, which is "going up to Israel," or they went illegally by Aliyah Bet.[13] The Israeli Consulate bought some of the boats. Some people were able to buy their way for cigarettes. Then the English stopped the Aliyah Bet boats and turned them back. One boat, the Exodus, that my cousins were on, went all the way to Haifa, and they turned them around and sent them all the way back to Hamburg. Then they went on another boat. The second time is was a smaller boat. And they ended up in Cyprus. They were in Cyprus for months and months.

Eisenhower had a Jewish rabbi and a judge that advised him about the conditions. I met the judge and his wife—actually he is from Rochester, New York and his name is Bernstein—they came to the Israeli Consulate. That was when the Aliyah Bet ship, Exodus, was caught and brought back to Hamburg. When all this happened, we told the judge's wife to call Hadassah in New York to ship clothes, and they called and sent telegraphs. Within days we got truckloads of clothing—you cannot imagine how much clothing came, and in such good condition.

When I worked for the Consulate in Frankfurt, I had inflammation of the ovaries. They first tried to treat it with diathermy. That didn't help, so they sent me to a hospital in Munich —a Catholic hospital with nuns. I was waiting for six weeks to get penicillin. Every time the penicillin came, they would sell it on the

13   Aliyah Aleph was the name for the limited Jewish immigration permitted by the British at this time. There was also illegal immigration by Jews to Palestine, called Aliyah Bet. From 1945 to 1948, the illegal immigration efforts were also called bricha—which was also the term for those who helped Jewish DPs move illegally across European borders. In 1947, the S.S. Exodus was boarded by a British patrol and forcibly returned to Europe. The ensuing publicity embarrassed the British government. [Wikipedia]

black market. When it came, you had to get it every four hours. The nuns would give you the shots. I was due to have it in the middle of the night. A nun—I called them sisters—came with a lantern, and I said, "Sister I had the last shot here." She said, "Shut up and turn over," and she gave me a shot in the same place. I have a lump to this day, and I'm always afraid I'm going to get cancer. When I was in the hospital, they brought me some Spam. We didn't have refrigerators, and I put it between the two windows to stay cold—we were by some double windows. I ate it, and by a miracle, I didn't get poisoned. I got extremely sick, but I didn't die. Spam is traif—non kosher.

After the treatment, they sent me to recover to a hotel in Berchtesgaden. I was sent from the camp, from the Consulate. Those young waitresses knew it and hated every appearance of mine. They knew I was Jewish. Hitler's Eagle's Nest was across the street from the hotel. When I got better, I got to go in the gilded elevator, and I went through the salt mine, and the tunnels where you sit on a piece of leather and slide down long slides.

Leaving Germany
Getting Papers

During those three years in Germany, I was working part of the time in the Zeilsheim and part of the time in Frankfurt. I came to the States in 1949, after everybody else from the family was here already. Uncle Louis had brothers in the United States, who had come earlier to make room for the children, and he had the privilege to come to the United States because he had brothers here. I was an orphan, so they considered I had no direct relatives, no one who could sponsor me. In the meantime, toward the end, I had a room in a house with a German family In Frankfurt. I paid rent in cigarettes from the Israeli Consulate. Then they closed the camp down, and they sent my papers to Kassel. I visited there when Hersi and Manyi were in Kassel. It's a northern town. A big city.

For three years I waited for the Czech quota to come to the United States. The Czech quota wasn't good—my cousin Manyi

Figure 14

Affidavits to affirm the identity of Lola Goldstein as Lea Müller.

left: full paper for internment in Auschwitz.

top below: detail of affidavit in English.

bottom below: detail of English section in separate affidavit, concerning Lea Müller's birthplace and birth date.

Affidavit

I hereby confirm and declare solemnly that I, Lea Müller, have been interned in the concentration - camp Auschwitz from May 21,1944 until January 18,1945. There the No. A - 5887 has been tattooed on my left lower arm. Thereafter I have been in the camps of Ravensbrück, Marchow and Leipzig, from where I was evacuated and liberated at Grimma by the American Troops.

We, the co-undersigned witnesses confirm solemnly, that we have been interned together with Miss. Müller in the concentration - camp Auschwitz. I, Dora Dzaba have been together with Miss Müller until our liberation.

Kassel, den 8. Dezember 1948

Affidavit

I hereby confirm and declare solemnly that according to official documents which I have seen but which are now destroyed, I Lea Müller have been born on May 5, 1927 at Dubrovo (Czechoslowakia).

The co-undersigned confirms solemnly the accuracy of the above statement. We know Miss Müller since her birth.

Kassel, den 8. Dezember 1948

even married a Russian Jewish man so she could come sooner. She said, "I married Seymour just on paper, because the Russian quota was good." Seymour Silberman was a man I knew in the DP Camp, and I introduced them. When she arrived in the US, the hosts provided one bedroom, and she said, "We are not married. It was just on paper." Later on they fell in love, and had a regular wedding. They had three successful children and a lot of grandchildren.

I was taken from camp to camp in Germany and worked throughout helping others to leave. Now I was even more wanting to come to the U.S. What did I have to do? I had to change my identity and take some papers of someone who had moved away to Israel. At my work, I made out false papers for people to go on the Aliyah Bet to Israel. They bought boats for cigarettes and for guns, and, and people either went through Marseilles or through Italy.

I knew this couple. They were engaged, and they wanted to go to Israel. So we made out false papers for them, so I knew that she was close in age and height and everything to me. Her name was Lea or Leah—sometimes there was an "h" on the end—Mueller [Müller]. The father's first name was Meyer. It is a Jewish name. I think her mother's maiden name was Herskowitz. I didn't tell them, but after they left, I took on the woman's identity; I took her papers. Then I applied to go to the United States. Finally Manyi and Hersi left for America, and I was the last one who left. I was the last one out of the DP camp. And I came to the U.S. on those false papers.

I didn't stay in Kassel, although my papers were there. Then they called me, and said that I should get ready for the trip. And when I went there, I had to see the Consul, and I was so scared. He had this paper, and he was left-handed. I thought he had rejected the whole paper, but he signed it with his left hand, and I was ready.

Ship to the USA

Then I took a ship. It was a ship that carried the military. We first were taken to Bremen, and we were supposed to leave from there. But it was very foggy, so we took a train to Hamburg and we finally left on February 13, 1949, on a different ship. It was called

Figure 15

Front cover and inside detail
of menu for special dinner
aboard the S. S. Marine
Shark, which brought Lola
Goldstein to the United
States in 1949.

Note handwritten
on the back page
of the menu,
by a shipboard
friend,
remembering
time shared
on the ship,
before separating
to enter new lives
when the ship
docked in
New York
the next day.

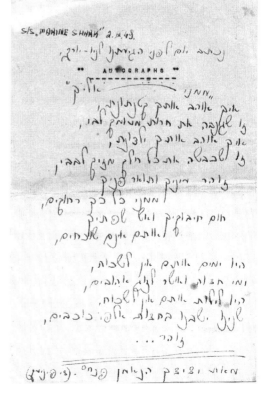

S.S. Marine Shark. [14] I didn't pay for my passage. I think they got money for it from the United Nations. I was in a big room on the ship—28 in one room. We had to stand in line to take a shower. When we went through the English Channel, it was so rough, they were closing off each section of the ship, and I said why is that, and they said it was because they still had torpedoes and they that if they were hit and one part of the ship is destroyed, it should be safe in the other part. Out of 500 on board, there were just a handful didn't get seasick. I was one. We had a big dinner on February 22, Presidents' Day. It was the day before we landed. Most people didn't want to come to the dining area because they were so sick. And there were hardly any people coming to dinner. The captain told me, tell the people that it is important for them to eat. They wouldn't be as sick if they ate. They sat on the open deck, covered with a blanket, and the blanket was full of salt from the spray. They said they don't care if they ever got to the United States. They just wanted to die. I was lucky. I remember, we had sort of a festive dinner, and when I was eating chicken, and the captain came to me and he said, "Even Queen Elizabeth picks up the bone"—the chicken bone—and they ate the meat right off the bone.

My Uncle Louis and Aunt Magda had sent me materials to make a camel hair coat with lining and thread and buttons. I will never forget it. They didn't have much, but they sent packages to us to Germany. I had the coat made, and I was wearing it when they met me. I wore that coat when I arrived in New York. Finally, I was in the U.S.

---

14   The S.S. Marine Shark was one of the ships converted by the United States Lines into troopships that were used by the US Navy to carry Displaced Persons from Europe to the US during the early postwar years. [Several Wikipedia articles and lists]. The menu from the Washington Birthday dinner gives details of the commander. The personal message on the back was a farewell message in Hebrew to "Lea" from Pinchas, who writes among other lines: "These are days we will remember when we were sitting and watching the stars."

Figure 16

Lola Goldstein
arrives in
New York,
March 1, 1949,
wearing the
coat made with
materials sent
to her in Germany
by her Uncle Louis
and Aunt Magda.

LEA MUELLER
48 Ashford St.
Brooklyn, N.Y.

BIRTHPLACE -   Dubrovc, Czechoslovakia

DATE OF BIRTH - May 5, 1927

MARITAL STATUS - Single

RESIDENCE - Presently living with Uncle, Mr. Louis Goldstein, at
        above address. Telephone number Applegate 7-8868.

EDUCATION - Hebrew Elementary School - 4 years

        Hebrew Reform Real Gymnasium, Mukacevo, Czechoslovakia, 8 yrs.
        Graduated in 1944.

1944 - Was taken to concentration camps in Poland and Germany
        with my parents and am the only survivor of my family.
        I remained in these concentration camps until the
        liberation in 1945.

1945 - 1947 I was sent to various D.P. camps in Germany where I
        worked as secretary to the Welfare Officer of UNRRA and also
        as Hebrew kindergarten teacher of the children in the camps.

1947 - 1948 Worked as secretary for the Jewish Agency for Palestine
        in Frankfort, Germany. My directors were Rachel Adiv and
        George I. Klompus.

QUALIFICATIONS - Proficient in speaking the following languages, as well
        as reading and writing them - Hebrew, English, Czech, German,
        Hungarian and Yiddish.

        I am also able to type in Hebrew and English.

Figure 17

Vita constructed by Lola for herself as Lea Müller,
for her job search in New York.

Part IV: Life in the United States

Work and Life in New York

I came on the ship to New York. We landed in New York—Ellis Island was closed. When I first saw the Statue of Liberty, I was so emotional I got seasick. I was never seasick before. We stopped at the Statue of Liberty, and the immigration agents came aboard and checked our papers. Then we arrived at the dock in New York, and Uncle Jake and Uncle Louis met me at the ship. They knew I was coming. I wrote to them from Bremen, in Germany, and told them what ship.

We had lunch in a drug store. Ben and Harry, Jake's sons, were there. The drug store had leather booths, and I had never experienced that before—that was unusual. Then we went to cousin Harry's office. Then I went to Uncle Louis and Aunt Magda's house, and I stayed in their apartment in Brooklyn for a while. Their daughter Susie was just a year old, and she was standing at the window and looking at what's happening.

Soon, I saw an ad for a job in the paper, I went in and applied, and was hired. So a few days after I arrived, I had a job working for the Levin Brothers Toy and Novelty Import Company across the street from the Flatiron Building. They were an export-import company, and they imported toys and novelties from Japan. People didn't mind buying from Japan because it was so cheap to buy. I remember that the ships used to come to Seattle and to San Francisco; and then the things came by truck or train. They equally did toys and notions. They were the only ones who had the merchandise to sell, and they shipped to Puerto Rico, Cuba—all the islands—and South America.

There were two brothers that owned the business. One was

לאמריקה-ארצ הישראלית הסוכנות
JEWISH AGENCY FOR PALESTINE
Head Office. U.S.Zone, Germany

Telephone: 48 13 73, 4 24 26

Munich, Maria-Theresia Str. 11
January 21, 1949

To whom it may concern:

This is to confirm that Miss Leah Miller has been working in our offices in Frankfurt from June 1947 until August 1948. She has fulfilled various tasks in the secretariate of the office, to our full satisfaction.

YJ/sr

ישראל-לארצ היהודית הסוכנות
JEWISH AGENCY FOR PALESTINE
FRANKFURT U.S. ZONE, GERMANY

Telephon: military 2 33 31, 21629
Nr. 269/49

Frankfurt/Main, Friedrichstraße 29
6. 2. 1949

TO WHOM IT MAY CONCERN:

This is to certify that Miss Lea MUELLER was employed as secretary of this Office from June 1, 1947 till August 10, 1948. Miss Mueller did her job excellently and we can recommend her warmly for such a position as she possesses the full knowledge of typewriting as well as the knowledge of the Hebrew, English, Hungarian, Czech, Yiddish and German languages.

She stopped working at this Office because of dissolving the department in which she was employed.

Georg I. Klompus
Jewish Agency for Palestine
Frankfurt U.S. Zone Germany

Figure 18

Two letters of recommendation from the Jewish Agency for Palestine in Frankfurt, for Lola as Leah Miller (Lea Mueller)

Philip, and the other was Isadore—they called him "I. L." . There were five brothers, and the other three were salesmen, on the road selling the merchandise. I got $7.50 a week. We checked the different companies' credit and what they made. There was a company called Dunn and Bradstreet. They had a huge book. I found the customer, and sent a note to the manager saying what the credit was of this company. We had fluorescent lights and my eyes got so bad from reading the fine print that eventually I had to start wearing glasses.

I stayed with Uncle Louis and Aunt Magda for a while. Aunt Magda once gave me some money to take to Macy's to make a payment on their furniture. First I went to the orange juicy lunch place around the corner, and I sat there. I had my wallet in my lap and, it was stolen. I couldn't pay, and the money Aunt Magda gave to me was also gone. I never told that to them. I had a friend, Vera, whose sister was in the United States from before the war. She borrowed the money and gave it to me, and I paid her $5 at a time to repay the $35.00 payment to Macy's.

Next I moved to Great Neck, New York, and stayed for a while with cousin Harry Goldstein and his wife Barbara and their three boys. My Uncle Jake had twin boys, and one of them was Harry. They were so kind to me, and the boys were very loving. I lived with them for several months. They took me places. For instance, Harry took me to his bridge club to see how they play bridge. I met their friends, who were all wonderful people. I am most grateful to them for helping me get settled in America. I was always very close with Barbara. During this time, I was working for the export-import company in Manhattan, and Harry frequently gave me a ride in his car to Manhattan. But most of the time, I would take the bus to the railway station, and take the Long Island Railroad to the city, and then a subway to work.

I stayed with Harry and Barbara for a bit even after their son, Alan, had polio. He had Sister Kenney helpers that came to massage him and gave him baths. Then I moved out. Harry and Barbara had a friend whose elderly mother lived in an apartment on Ocean Avenue in Brooklyn. She spent the winters in Florida

DPC—217
(4-4-49)

DISPLACED PERSONS COMMISSION

WASHINGTON 25, D. C.

April 25, 1949

Dear Sir or Madam,

The Congress of the United States has established the Displaced
Persons Commission to select for immigration to this country, persons
displaced as a result of World War II. Under the principles laid
down by the Congress, you were among those selected.

The Congress is interested in how displaced persons fare after
settling in the United States. So that the Congress may be kept informed on this matter, it requires that you provide certain factual
information.

The information is to be provided twice a year, for two years.
The dates for reporting are January 1 and July 1 of each year. The
first report is due on the next reporting date after you have been
in this country 60 days or more. Forms for these reports are provided
by the Displaced Persons Commission.

Since, according to our records, you entered the United States
on or before May 1, 1949, you are required to report on July 1, 1949.
You may mail your report to us on or after June 15, 1949, but it must
be mailed by June 30, 1949.

The form to be used in making your report is enclosed, as is a
return envelope which requires no postage. Forms to be used by you
for future reports will be available in local offices of the U. S.
Immigration and Naturalization Service, approximately 45 days ahead
of the reporting date.

You are urged to submit reports on the dates specified, since
there are criminal penalties, upon conviction thereof, for willful
failure to report.

Sincerely,

Ugo Carusi, Chairman

Edward M. O'Connor

Harry N. Rosenfield

Figure 19

U.S. Displaced Persons Commission
letter of welcome, with details of requirements
for submission of annual information form.

and the summers in the Catskills. I sublet from her. Most of the time, I had a beautiful apartment all to myself. I didn't cook. I had a friend that didn't have any children at that time yet, so she cooked, and I paid her for the dinners and ate at her place.

While working, I went to classes in a high school for a while, where I learned shorthand. Then I went to Brooklyn College and took English and literature. I paid for this with earnings from my job. I spent two and one half years in New York. But life was increasingly difficult in New York. I could not take the difficult times taking the subway. I used to pass out in the summertime because of the air, and it was body-to-body.[1] I passed out, and people walked over me, and somebody took me to the bathroom, and then I went to work where they said, "Take a taxi and go home." I was trying to get a different job with some Jewish organizations, but they said that I wasn't qualified enough. So I moved to Detroit.

Move to Detroit

By this time Uncle Louis and Aunt Magda had come to Detroit, because my cousin Harry's twin brother, Ben, lived there with his wife, Edna. Ben was comptroller in a chain of department stores—Winkelman's—in Detroit. Ben helped Uncle Louis get a job with that firm. So I came, and I lived again for a while with Uncle Louis and Aunt Magda, and their child, Susan. Then I got a one-room apartment on Boston Avenue. I went to Wayne State University for a year when I came to Detroit, and I was active in the student activities at Wayne.

Work with Ruth Adler Schnee

Ben's wife, Edna Goldstein, worked at Winkelman's with Uncle Louis. Edna helped design the interiors of the Winkelman stores. Ruth Adler Schnee[2] and her husband, Eddie Schnee, supplied the

---

1   Lola's daughter, Ruth Taubman, remembers always being struck by the fact that the stifling, packed subway cars overwhelmed her mother, because they were so reminiscent of the boxcars to Auschwitz.

2   The Ruth Adler Schnee interview in The Archives of American Art

materials and the plan of what to do. Edna helped me get a job with Ruth Adler Schnee. I was one of her first employees.

Ruth Adler was born in Germany, in Düsseldorf. Her mother, Marie Adler, was a student of the Bauhaus, and the family was very artistic. They escaped the Holocaust in the 30's and came to Detroit. Ruth Adler went to Cass Tech High School in Detroit and then to Rhode Island School of Design. After she graduated, she became a judge of the Scholastic Art Awards for students. She met Eddie Schnee, a graduate of Yale. They married and founded their design business. Ruth Adler Schnee designed the cloth, and Eddie hand-printed it with silkscreen. Eddie was very kind, very knowledgeable. And he was very nice and helpful to me.

Their business was open maybe a year before I came. They printed drapery material for the Ford Rotunda, which eventually burned down. Ruth Adler Schnee also had a lot of private customers. The business was on Puritan Avenue near 6 and 7 Mile, separate from their home. Her office was in the front, and the screen-printing was in the back. It wasn't big, but she had a nice showroom, where she displayed crystal and dishes and different materials. She made pillows for people, for the living room, and it was nice.

They were very nice. I didn't drive. They used to pick me up for work, and we were very friendly. I used to baby sit for them, for their children. When I came there, Ruth Adler Schnee had one other lady, Trudy Ehrenfeld, working for her in the business. I did all kinds of things in the store. I helped in the office, filling orders, and ordering things from the different manufacturers. And, if customers came, I helped them. I worked with Trudy Ehrenfeld. I worked for their business for two and one-half years.

Business was good. There was a boom in Detroit after the war. The factories were building cars, and people were building homes

---

at the Smithsonian in Washington, available on the web at http://www.aaa. si.edu/collections/interviews/oral-history-interview-ruth-adler-schnee-12111, includes information on Ben and Edna Goldstein, their Yamasaki house, and the nature of the Ruth Adler Schnee and Eddie Schnee business in Detroit during these years.

and apartments, so they came to Adler Schnee. The Taubman family were builders. They were building homes for themselves and came to her for help, and we furnished their homes. Al Taubman's wife, Reva, came. They were building a house. Her mother was also building a house. So I met Reva first. Then my in-laws built a house, too, not far away—6 Mile and 7 Mile Road—or maybe it was 7 Mile and 8 Mile—near Outer Drive; and we helped furnish that newly built house. Another Taubman brother built himself a home, and we furnished that, and I met that sister-in-law. So I met Sam's parents and his brothers and sisters-in-law before I met Sam.

Meeting Sam Taubman

We were busy, and Sam was the last one to come. He was actually pretty new in town, too. His sister, Goldye, had talked him into coming to Detroit. She had a small hotel. On the main floor, there was a tenant, and she gave them notice to leave, so Sam could open a shower door business there.

Sam was a multitalented man. I can't tell enough about him. He was well read. He studied a lot. He built his first shower doors with his own hands, and he went and measured openings for shower doors and tub enclosures. He built them himself and installed them himself. His shower doors were the best. He invented the piano hinge on them, and they were all custom-built. He had anodized shower doors, and some were in gold tones. He also did some cast aluminum grilles, for the car companies that had to be anodized. Sam also designed mirrored closet doors.

After a while, his father built him a factory and an office on Wyoming Avenue near 5 Mile Road to do the shower doors. In front was the office. Sam came to Ruth Adler Schnee when they were decorating the office, to furnish it. His brother, Al, designed these bookshelves. Sam had them built-in, and he had for many years a desk that was designed by his brother. One end of the desk was attached to the wall.[3] Most of the things for the new office, Sam

---

3   Lola's daughter, Ruth, now has this desk in her kitchen. The full story of who designed this remarkable desk remains a mystery. Perhaps it was the combined idea of Al Taubman, Sam Taubman, and Ruth Adler Schnee.

did over the telephone, but he did come finally to Adler Schnee, and I met him. We liked each other, and we exchanged phone numbers. He was sort of nervy. I remember he called me a few days before New Year's and wanted to take me out. I said, "Sorry, I'm busy." I don't remember if I was busy or not, but after New Year's, we were dating.

We didn't date very long, because he was 38 years old and I was 26, and I thought, "I'm going to remain an old maid." He kept taking me out. And he said, "You don't know, you are too young, but we're not going to go together too long, and we're going to get married." My in-laws had an anniversary. Sam's sister, Goldye had a party for her parents. I was invited. Sam and I had decided that at the party we would announce that we were engaged.

Sam's Early Life

Sam's parents, Philip and Fannie, had entered the country in Galveston, Texas. Fannie had a sister living in Davenport, Iowa, so they settled there. Philip got a job in Davenport building cars. Sam was born in Davenport, Iowa, on August 17, 1915. Sam didn't have a birth certificate. It wouldn't have been important when he was born to get a birth certificate. Many years later, when we were trying to get a passport when we were traveling, Sam had to find some people who were alive when he was born, so they could certify, and he could get a passport.

When Sam was five years old, the whole family moved to Pontiac. Eventually, there were four children. Goldye was the oldest. Then came Sam. Then came Lester. And Alfred was the baby. When he was a young boy, Sam was always making little airplanes. When his family went to a picnic, he didn't go. He stayed in the basement working on boats, working on airplanes. His father wasn't very nice about it. Sometimes he would smash the things Sam made, because Sam didn't want to go to the picnic with his family.

In Pontiac, Sam's father was studying real estate. Eventually he was in the building business. He started it when Al was young. So Sam grew up in Pontiac. He had a hard life, because it was the Depression. He went to grade school and high school. And while he was in high school, he was working. He was caddying at a restricted club's golf course. A Jewish person was not even allowed to go into the caddies' room there, so he had to eat his sandwich under a tree outside. He also worked at Sears Roebuck, lifting heavy stuff, even though he was skinny and tall. His sister Goldye worked for a dentist. She administered gas, without any training. And she, too, worked for Sears for a while.

When Sam graduated high school, he went to the University of Michigan to study aeronautical engineering. He rented a room in the attic of a house. He didn't have access to a shower, so he had to go shower at the sports facility. He must have had some food, but his mother sent additional food.[4] In between terms and most weekends, he hitchhiked home to work at Sears.

When Sam graduated in 1940, he got a position as assistant to a professor, to teach classes in aeronautical engineering. He also taught classes in metallurgy and mathematics. Then he moved to California and went to work for Lockheed. He also taught extension courses in mathematics at UCLA.

He had lots of girlfriends with whom he corresponded. Women wrote to him and he replied. There was, especially, one young lady, and I don't know what happened, but she married somebody else, and she died young of cancer. But he kept in contact with her parents. They lived in Texas and later on in Hollywood. So when we were married, and we went to Texas and later to Hollywood, we would look up the mother.

In California, Sam was increasingly anxious to go in the Air Force. He was advised that it was more important for him to teach ground training to pilots. Then it was the last year of the war, and they didn't need any more pilots, so he was allowed to join the Navy. He did communications on the aircraft carrier USS Randolph outside of Washington D.C., protecting Washington. And he had quite a social life in Washington. He had dates, and all the women were after him.

---

4   Sam had meals at the Michigan Union, and showered at Waterman Gym.

After the war, Sam enjoyed flying glider planes from the airport at Frankfurt, Michigan.[5] He told me how they were pulling him with a regular plane into the air, and then they released the glider. He enjoyed that. Later, when the children were young, we took them to Frankfurt, and Sam showed them where he used to fly. The children were so proud of him.

Married Life

Wedding

When we got married. I didn't have anything. My husband bought my wedding gown and all my clothes.[6] Sam and I got married in Ben and Edna's house in Birmingham.[7] The twin brothers, Ben and Harry (still in Great Neck, New York), made the wedding together. It was a very small wedding—maybe 40 people—on March 28, 1954. There was a luncheon, and we had an accordion player. We had a rabbi and a cantor marry us. Many years later, there was an announcement in the Orlando paper that a cantor was coming to sing for the holidays. He had an unusual name, and when we checked, he turned out to be the son of the cantor who took part in our wedding.

We went on honeymoon to Jamaica. We took an airplane and flew to Miami and slept overnight. The next day we took a smaller plane. We had to make a stop in Cuba to refuel. Then we went on to Jamaica for a honeymoon—a very nice vacation. Sam was so hardworking, that while I was sitting on the beach, he was working and sending by mail his designs back to the United States.

---

5   Lola's daughter, Ruth, recalls that Sam actually earned his pilot's license at the age of 15. Later, Sam became skilled enough to solo over Lake Michigan from the Frankfurt airfield, from which he glided many times.

6   Lola notes that on the wedding papers, she records Leah's birthdate and age because, "Actually 'Leah' was two years younger than 'Lola,' so on the original paper, I was two years younger than my true age."

7   Lola's daughter, Ruth, notes that Ben and Edna's house in Birmingham was the first house that Minoru Yamasaki ever designed.

Figure 20

Lola and Sam Taubman after their wedding.
Birmingham, Michigan, March 25, 1954.

Life in the Detroit Area

When Sam's parents moved from Pontiac to Detroit, they built a home on Monica, near Outer Drive. It was a nice house, but there was no bedroom for Sam. They built just a one-bedroom house to force Sam to move out on his own. That's when Sam started his business, and got the one-bedroom apartment.

Sam liked to cook, so he had a one-bedroom apartment with a living room with a closet that was the kitchen. On the top was a little oven and the bottom was the refrigerator. When we came back from the honeymoon, we lived there, but not too long, because my brothers-in-law, they are all builders.

Goldye's husband was building duplexes on Meyers Road. So we moved into one of the duplexes. We had a neighbor, another family that lived next to us, and they eventually bought the building. I remember the lady was Catholic, and she went to church at six in the morning every day. And the children had to look out for themselves, and they went to Catholic school and they came home for lunch. I remember the little girl telling me that for lunch they had cheese with broth with oil and vinegar. It's an Italian specialty, with fresh bread.

We lived there only one year. Alyssa was born while we lived in that duplex. Then my brother-in-law, Lester, built homes in Southfield near 10 Mile and Greenfield. And we bought one of the first houses there, on Maryland. It was nice—a tri-level with bedrooms upstairs, just a few steps up, then the main level, and a few steps further down was a family room. And on that level, we had a separate bedroom for help. I had the children, so we often had help. I didn't have a sister or a brother, and my sisters-in-law were not about to help me. I was able to get some help because we could provide quarters for them. I knew a lady when Ruthie was a baby. She came and she stayed with us for several years. She was from Tennessee, and she had a daughter in the Grosse Pointe area. So she visited her daughter on weekends. She was very helpful. She made little curtains for the bathroom. And she made little aprons for the children. We called her Mrs. Lynch.

Then, when Mrs. Lynch could no longer do it, from time to time, there were German refugees that were looking for jobs. So we had one, then another one. Once we had, just for the weekend, a black lady. That was unfortunate because while we were out, she had her boyfriend come over, and she wasn't very young. They drank our liquor, and when we came home, our baby was still in the buggy, not put to bed. They could have burned the house down. Sam was so upset that he said, "Pack up and leave now, at midnight." And she said, "But he's gone." That's how we found out that she had somebody there. Nervy. So that was that.

Then we had a daytime helper, and we were missing something of Sam's. He had coins, and she took them. When we couldn't find them, we called her mother, and the mother came over, and the daughter told her that she put the coins under her pillow. So she stayed one night, and that was it. Then I managed by myself.

We moved from that tri-level in the town of Southfield to the community of Bingham Farms (a bedroom community, one square mile) in Birmingham. The community was originally a farm. There we lived in a two-story house built by Lester. We lived in that house from 1970 to 1981. It was a nice house, beautiful trees. It was interesting that when my brother-in-law built the house, his wife Adele, who decorated his model homes, asked if I would come and help her select some colors for one of the models. She was very talented. She was a graduate of the Art Institute of Chicago. Of the sisters-in-law, I was the friendliest with her. Little did I know that we would end up buying that house, so as it happened, I liked the colors. We had olive green woodwork and daffodil yellow carpeting.

We had a good time in that house. It was never completely furnished, and never had too many accessories, but it wasn't that important. Richard became a Bar Mitzvah when we lived there. When Alyssa was confirmed, we had a party. But it was hard for me with the children.

Figure 21

Sam and Lola Taubman family. Top: Lola Taubman with Richard,
Ruthie, and Alyssa, 1960. Middle: Sam Taubman with Alyssa,
Ruthie, and Richard, 1961. Bottom: Ruthie, Richard, and Alyssa.

I played Mah Jongg once a week the entire time I lived in the Detroit area. I started playing Mah Jongg when we lived in Southfield, with the children in their pajamas attending all the steps of the game, and listening how we called it. We played each session in someone else's house. And we played from 8 pm to 1 am.

When I left Detroit, my group gave me a set, but I never used it. At first I didn't find anyone in Florida to play. I finally did have a group in Florida and played until I came back to Michigan in 2005. When I was in California, Alyssa played Mah Jongg with a group, so I joined them. And they were so surprised—I hadn't played since I moved to Ann Arbor in 2005, and I beat them all.

I was busy with the children as they were growing up. They had performances, either singing or dancing. The girls took dancing lessons in Royal Oak. They were not very good at dancing. I would take them for rehearsals. Alyssa started early with her music. She took piano lessons from the time she was 6½. She had private lessons with Miss (Maryan) Fleisher (Abramsohn), a very good teacher. Alyssa always kept in touch with her piano teacher, who had students into her nineties. Alyssa was one of her favorite students. She did well. The teacher had a studio in the basement. Each year she had a recital, and Alyssa was always the last to play. From an early age, Alyssa went to Interlochen[8] in the summer. The nicest time was visiting her and listening to the concerts. When she was a teenager, we bought Alyssa a Steinway piano, and then she went to music school at the University of Michigan.

While Alyssa was at Interlochen, Ruthie and Richard went to day camp and then overnight camp. In high school, Ruthie also went to Interlochen for two summers. When he was in high school, Richard went on a two-week camping trip, once. They were allowed only to take a pair of shorts and a tee shirt. They were

---

8   Interlochen was founded in 1928, near Traverse City, Michigan, as The National Music Camp. It has since expanded into the renowned Interlochen Center for the Arts and Interlochen Arts Camp. Young students come each summer for intensive study sessions in music, and now also in art, dance, theater, writing, and motion picture arts.

Figure 22

Sam and Lola Taubman Family Homes.
Top: Home on Maryland in Southfield, MI (1957-1970).
Middle: Home on Britner in Bingham Farms, MI (1970-1981).
Bottom: Home on Riverbend Blvd. in Longwood, Florida.

riding by bus to Canada, and they had to carry a canoe overhead, and they cooked, and they had to clean up wherever they were.

The children went to Hebrew School several days a week after school, as well as to Sunday School at our temple, a Reform Temple. Then Richard began to study for his Bar Mitzvah, and Alyssa was confirmed. So there was driving to the temple; I was busy all the time. Ruthie didn't like our temple's confirmation program, so she joined Adat Shalom Synagogue that my in-laws had belonged to, on 13 Mile Road. They had a nice congregation. So Ruthie took their confirmation class. It was a very small program. They had nine girls in the class.

Sam and I went to some concerts. Not for the whole series, but some of them. And I took the children to the art museum [Detroit Institute of Arts] when there was something special going on. They had puppet shows and children's plays in the theater. I only had a Chevrolet. Sam said, "You want wheels. You got wheels." No air conditioning, no clock. Nothing—just a stripped-down model. Before that, I was grocery shopping with Alyssa, with a buggy, on buses; I had to wait a long time before Sam could come and pick us up. It wasn't easy. Some things, I had luxuries. Other things, I didn't.

Changes in Detroit

Things were going bad in Detroit. We had the riots, and the unions were after Sam to unionize his people. I was so fearful, because Sam had a strange schedule. He would get up late, so the children complained they never had breakfast with him. As much as he had wonderful qualities, he was so busy making a living and working hard—work was his life; he didn't spend much time with the children. He got up late, had breakfast, went to work, and worked until after closing time. So the children could not be like other children, and have early dinner and play after dinner. We had to wait and have dinner at seven, sometimes 7:30, and after dinner, he had to have a nap.

When he got up, he went back to the city to work in his office every night. Every night. Sometimes he would come home at three and four o'clock in the morning. His reason for going back was so he could design things so his factory workers could start producing them in the morning. That was his schedule. As things were getting bad, one night I went back with him. And the union "goons"— the organizers—were with guns across the street. Things were so bad. The neighborhood became so decayed, and later, a few doors down from the factory, there was a nightclub, and the mayor's brother got shot dead.

Florida

Life in Florida

Sam had a customer, John Wall, who was in the aluminum business. And he was a very good customer. He had a very nice house. We visited their house and knew them. He was a Seventh-day Adventist, and he knew of Orlando. He and his wife had been there and looked around, and they must've had some friends there. He had already moved to Florida part-time, and was building a factory. So he convinced Sam to join him. In 1981, Sam had to dismantle his factory and move all his machinery to Florida, because he was going to continue with designing and manufacturing shower doors there. It was a very hard move. Several trucks had to carry the equipment. When Sam closed his business in Detroit in 1981, he still had his first employee who had worked for him since 1948.

In 1980-1981, Sam used to commute to Florida from Detroit, while he helped the partner, John Wall, design and finish the building, because Sam needed special things. First of all, they built a foundry. They would buy scrap aluminum and melt it down, and turn it into billets. They bought extrusion machines and equipment. Sam was so busy supervising the building of the foundry. Then he designed a brand-new anodizing plant and shower door factory, and they built them from the ground up. It took a lot of effort.

Sam worked with his partner at their company, Florida Extrusion, which was located in Sanford, off of Airport Road, on

Jewett Lane. Sam developed the shower door division within the company, and they manufactured shower doors.

When we came to Florida and looked for a house. Sweetwater Oaks was just being developed in Longwood, Florida, near Sanford. We had a realtor and she took us around. She said you don't want to live in The Springs; it is too mixed-up there. They have condominiums and houses and homes and everything. She brought us to the place we settled. We didn't want a pool. She sold us some blueprints. This house wasn't built; just the two-by-fours were up.

On our flight back to Michigan after we bought the house, Sam made changes to the plans during the flight in the airplane, and called in the changes when we got back to Detroit.[9] One of the changes Sam made was to turn the bedroom closest to the front door into a library. The original plan had that bedroom with a door that opened across from a bathroom. Sam closed that door off and cut the "bedroom" closet in half, so he could put in double doors to open from the library into the foyer. Sam moved the bookshelves that he had had in his Detroit office, and attached them to the library wall. When those bookshelves ran out of room, Sam designed additional bookcases in cherry, and ordered them, and they were built.

Had we been in Florida while the house was being finished, our kitchen would have been different. We would've had an exit to the porch, and the kitchen would have been reversed. We bought the house in 1980 and moved in in 1981. The winters were hard in Michigan. When we were moving to Florida, it was 10 below zero, and we had over a foot of snow. The moving trucks couldn't pull onto the driveway. We had to carry everything out to the street. The children were already out of college, so we didn't have to move with the children, but they came and visited us often.

---

9   Longwood and Sanford are both near Orlando, Florida. Lola's daughter, Ruth, remembers that the builder in Longwood adopted many of Sam's changes into standard features of the other homes being built in the Sweetwater Oaks development.

Figure 23

Lola and Sam
Taubman,
on their 30th
Wedding
Anniversary.
Longwood,
Florida.
March 28,
1984.
Photo by
Ruth
Taubman.

In Florida, Sam did some work for Winn–Dixie. They made carts—not the carts that you shop with, but the carts they use to bring in things from the warehouse to stock up the store. Sam built those. He also designed camouflage-patterned tubing for arrow shafts for the arrow companies.

In Detroit, Sam's shower doors were all custom-built. In Florida, they were more mass-produced. The company in Florida sold extrusions for shower doors to glass companies. They had a lot of employees. His partner was too trusting, and some employees stole a lot of things. You would think, what can they steal in aluminum? Well they made trades. They sold the aluminum to somebody who could build them a swimming pool. Especially there were two brothers, and they bought everybody Christmas gifts. I have a ceramic box that they bought us.

Things were going bad, and it was just too much, too much. The partner, John Wall, wanted to leave. He was older than Sam, and he had a son that wasn't very successful. So they sold the building and the business. First to the Pritzkers, who owned an airline (Braniff), and the Hyatt hotel chain (with the big hotel at Disney World). They also owned aluminum factories, and they had a man, Joel Lehman, that ran one of their factories in Erie, Pennsylvania, and he was a very smart man. He was originally an accountant. They would buy plants overseas and all kinds of things. They sent a man over and he decided it was a good deal for the company, so the Pritzkers bought that plant. They expanded, and they started building aluminum windows. They didn't want to continue with shower doors, because windows were easier and faster. They had a machine where they put aluminum billets in and extruded. They did extrusions, but not big; these were the ordinary-size windows, for when they built a whole apartment block or something. Then the Pritzkers sold it to this man, Joel. He bought it, and Sam remained as a consulting engineer and worked for them for years. Then Sam tapered off, and we were able to start traveling. We never traveled before. We had nice times traveling around the world.

Later while we were living in Florida, Sam was practically retired, but he still regularly gave engineering advice to Florida

Extruders. In the early 1990s, when his brother Al Taubman, purchased his first private jet, which was built by Gulfstream in Savannah, Georgia, he hired Sam to supervise the building of the airplane. Sam commuted to Savannah for a while. Eventually, we both lived in Savannah in a hotel for several weeks at the time, coming back and forth to Orlando to check on our house. This continued for a year. The people of Savannah were so nice and welcomed us into their community. We made friends there through the Temple. I played Mah Jongg with them and was active in the local chapter of Hadassah. When Al Taubman bought his second and third Gulfstream jets, they were built in Savannah, but finished in Appleton, Wisconsin. So we spent some time living in Appleton as well.

Retirement in Florida

We enjoyed our retirement years in Orlando. Sam and I enjoyed taking long walks together, and we ate dinner out frequently. I made friends quickly. I joined organizations, and we joined a temple. First we belonged to a liberal temple for about five years. Then we moved to Ohev Shalom. Sam wasn't much of a temple goer, so I went with friends. I participated in lighting candles every year at the Holocaust Center's Yom Hashoah service held in the JCC building. Sam and I also supported the fund-raising events at the Holocaust Center. And I went to talk to schools about my experiences. Sam played golf, and I continued to be involved with Hadassah and the synagogue, and played Mah Jongg with my good friends. We had many good friends: Gert and Jack Freeman, Sig and Marilyn Goldman, Gloria and Bill Goodman, Vera Fekete, and our wonderful neighbors, Jeanette and Grover Todd. I was also very close friends with Helen Greenspun, who is also a survivor and very active speaking in schools.

Sam and I started to travel extensively with friends and on our own. With friends, we traveled to northern and southern Europe, and on cruises in the Caribbean and through the Panama Canal. We also took a six-week tour to Australia, China, Singapore,

Indonesia, and Thailand. In Australia, we met my cousin Sam Moss and his family. His mother and my mother were sisters.

Snapshots of Family

Portrait of Sam

Sam passed away unexpectedly on December 15, 2004. We were married for over 50 years, although when we got married, people said our marriage wouldn't last. Sam had little health problems, but not major ones. As a matter of fact, he drove home two hours before he died. He was misdiagnosed by two doctors. I guess I should be thinking that it was his time to go.

I am not a doctor, but I know if someone has a chest pain and pain in the left arm, the first thing you do is have a cardiogram. Our doctor was a cardiologist, and he said since Sam had a stress test in July, in December he is still okay. So he sent Sam home instead of to the hospital. Then we went to another doctor because we thought maybe it was something to do with the digestive system. This doctor didn't know him. First the nurse wouldn't give him an appointment the next day, because they don't know the difference between an emergency and just a checkup. So we had to wait another day to see the doctor, and since he didn't know Sam, he says, "Well you look all right. Have some tests." And that was the end.

Our neighbors, Jeanette and Grover Todd, and our friends, Gert and Jack Freeman, were unbelievably kind to me during this difficult time. The children, Alyssa, Richard, and Ruth, came down to Florida and I returned with them to Michigan for Sam's funeral and burial. The funeral was a beautiful service, with all our old friends and family attending. We sat Shiva at Richard's home. About two weeks later, I returned to Florida with my children for a memorial service for Sam. The children each spoke beautifully about Sam. Sam had a strong will with the children and with me, but he was the best person I ever knew. I will miss him as long as I live.

Sam liked to live well. He liked good food, good clothes. He liked to stay in nice places. And most important of all, he was the cleanest human being I have ever met. He loved good clothes. He loved to be with the children. All the brains in the children came from him. They are mechanically minded. The girls are like men, like boys. They can fix anything. Alyssa and Ruthie are so independent. They make the decisions, both of them. Unfortunately, we didn't spend enough time with them, because they lived far from Florida, in Michigan and California. We tried to go to California twice a year and to Michigan at least twice a year, so I should be thankful that we had a good life, and that we were able to do some of the things.

Sam would sometimes procrastinate. Don't do anything today that you can do tomorrow. He was a very detailed man. His brother used to say, "Sam you can't see the forest for the trees." He was a product of the depression, so very frugal and sometimes mistrusting the system, because he went through that. I would say he had a hard beginning of life. He started working at age 10 as a caddie in a golf club; at 15, he worked for Sears; at one time he was selling men's clothes. When he went to college, tuition wasn't expensive and he was a good student. He must've had scholarships. As a matter of fact, he worked for a year after graduating high school before he went to college.

Sam had a sense of humor. Richard and Alyssa sent him faxes with jokes, lawyer jokes, and all kinds of things. He saved these, and they were so funny. He had favorite people, favorite restaurants. When we went to California, there was a restaurant, Buckeye Roadhouse, (between Alyssa's and downtown San Francisco). They had his favorite thing of calves' liver with sautéed onions and garlic mashed potatoes. They were so busy they took reservations six months in advance. But when Alyssa called that we were there, they took us. We would eat with the grandchildren. Our son-in-law used to love s'mores for dessert. We had nice times in California.

Figure 24

Lola and Sam Taubman, celebrating their
50th Wedding Anniversary, during visit to Michigan.
Photo taken on April 25, 2004.

Memories of Philip Taubman

My father-in-law, Philip Taubman, had a habit of going and buying four kosher chickens at the same time. And my mother-in-law, Fannie, had to stand and cook and bake. She liked to bake plain cookies. She died in 1960 at age 70. She was sick for quite a while.

My father-in-law remarried, in Florida. There are these coffee stands in Miami, and women would rent a cabana by the beach so they could see the men. (We called them in our families, "a natural blonde after fifty-five.") This lady, Sandra, was one, and she wasn't very nice. She was very ordinary, from Brooklyn. They were married for 13 years, and Philip passed away at 87. He came alone from Florida for Richard's Bar Mitzvah. Philip wasn't very smart about the stuff that he owned. He and Fannie had a custom-furnished house—Ruth Adler Schnee did it. Custom-made bedroom set and good furniture and good lamps. Sandra sold it all before she and Philip moved to Florida. If she could get $5 for a lamp, she took it. Whatever she could sell, she sold to get the money. And she burned all the family pictures. The only thing that Sandra didn't get hold of was a motel in Detroit near Northland. That was left for the grandchildren. Later Sandra moved to California and eventually died.

The Children

Richard was the first of our children to get married. The girls were more into professions, and they delayed. Both Alyssa and Ruth were 33 when they got married. Alyssa didn't have a child until she was 39, and has two girls. Ruth had a child within a year after she got married, and has two boys. Richard has two girls.

When Alyssa graduated high school, she went to the University of Michigan. She applied to the music school and she had to perform as a test. She took piano, composition, and music theory. In eight years, she did three degrees. She graduated from music school, psychology, and law. When Alyssa finished law school, they picked her for a job with a big law firm in Los Angeles. Later, she worked for Salomon Brothers. Now she's a lawyer and in real estate. Alyssa's husband is an attorney, and he commutes to the city every day. His name is Robert Rothman. They live in Ross, north of San Francisco beyond the Golden Gate Bridge.

Alyssa's two children are very smart. The big one is Talia, and the younger one is Mia. They have all the advantages that they can give them. They took both ballet and drama. Alyssa doesn't play piano in public now, but her older daughter, Talia, is just as talented, and they play duets. Talia has a good teacher. At Interlochen, Talia took drama (instead of piano) because her teacher didn't want her to be confused with the different method. Alyssa's little one, Mia, was taking chess lessons at age 6. Now, Mia is a fantastic artist and mathematician.

Richard is an attorney. At one point, all three of our children were at the University of Michigan at the same time. Alyssa finished her undergraduate work a year earlier than Richard, and then began law school at Michigan. Richard didn't want to go to law school at Michigan, because he didn't want to be compared to Alyssa, so he went to Boston University. When he graduated, he realized there were too many law schools in the Boston area, and it would be hard to find a job, so he came back to Michigan. Meanwhile, Sam and I moved to Florida before the house was sold, so Richard stayed in our Michigan house while he was studying for the bar. He likes Michigan, and thank God, he is successful. He is hard working and he does well. He specializes in real estate law. He takes care of shopping centers or people that buy land and develop businesses. He deals with all kinds of people. He specializes in zoning. He wrote a book in 2004 and presented it at a conference. Then he revised the book, and there was another conference.

Richard has two children—Rachel and Danielle. Both girls are beautiful, smart, and talented. Rachel is so artistic and Danielle is too, and good students—all 'A' students. Danielle played the viola. We bought her a viola. We gave her the money when she was Bat Mitzvah, and she saved it because at that time she was too little to have a full-size instrument, so she just rented one. The first year Rachel went to college, she was in the dorm, and she was so lucky to have a room by herself. Before school ended that year, she got together with a group of other girls and they rented a house. That's what they do now; they don't tear down the old houses. They have little porches on the front, and they like it better than being in the dorm. I don't know what they do about food. Probably they cook or eat out. There are so many eating places—delicatessens. Rachel befriended a rabbi's wife, and she learned from her how to cook. She ate at Hillel, and sometimes at the rabbi's place. She spent a summer in Israel with a group.

When Ruth went to the University of Michigan, she studied art, and within the School of Art, she specialized in metalsmithing, which is part of jewelry making. She had a wonderful Japanese metalsmithing professor, Hiroko Sato Pijanowski. Later, Ruth worked for the jewelry designer, David Yurman, in New York. She lived in Hoboken, but she commuted by subway. She worked for him for a year. His wife was a painter on her own. He was a designer, but he wasn't much of a businessman. So Ruthie was his production manager. Then she figured if she could run his business for him, she could run her own, and she became independent. Ruth and a classmate of hers from art school, Eve Peterson, started a little business. First they made jewelry and leather belts with beautiful buckles. They were both the designers and the craftsmen. When the partner got married and had children, they parted company. Then Ruth started out with custom jewelry. She bought different stones and made earrings and rings and bracelets. Then Ruthie had a little studio in Manhattan on 17th St. near Fifth Avenue, and started making things and selling the jewelry.

Ruth's husband, Bill MacConnel, works in a software company. She and Bill have two boys, Henry and Jack. Her son Henry was born in New York, while she lived in a "dump". It was in an old building maybe three stories high—a walk-up. You could see the Empire State Building right across. When Henry started crawling, I was afraid he was going to hurt himself; the linoleum had holes, and a window was broken. After a couple of years, they moved to Ann Arbor. They stored the furniture they had and lived in a furnished apartment. Then they bought this house on a very unusual flag-shaped lot. The other houses are close to the road and theirs is set back. What attracted them was the separate little building on the property that Ruth uses as a studio. The man who built the house built the separate building as a bomb shelter with all kinds of intricate exits. Anyhow, it worked out fine. Ruth has a beautiful studio and has three or four employees now. She works very hard. She travels, and has shows all over. In Ann Arbor, she has a show before Christmas and one in June.

You should see the collection of recordings of her children's performances that Ruthie has. Jack is playing the guitar. And Henry is also. Henry has such a good ear that they bought him a keyboard. Now he has a computer, and he composes and records on it. He played the French horn in the middle school band. Henry is so sensitive, that when the band teacher, who wasn't very smart, praised one student who played the best, and was mean to the others, that was enough for Henry not to want to continue with band class. He still is very good at computers. Henry and Jack, when they come home, the first thing they go to is the computer. Jack is cute, and smart—both children are darling.

All the grandchildren are darling. Richard's daughter is the oldest. Then comes Ruthie's children. Then comes Alyssa's children. The children know all of my story, but the grandchildren don't. The older grandchildren know some it, not all of it. All the children are very loving, and they were close to my husband and to me too. They try to take good care of me.

All the grandchildren are wonderful children. They are smart, they are nice people, talented, and the parents are doing a great job of raising them. Our children pay attention to their children. They help them with their homework. They take them to nice places. Our sons-in-law are good men; both work hard.

Back to Michigan and Ann Arbor

After Sam's death, my children and I decided I should move to Michigan, so I put our Longwood house up for sale. My children traveled back and forth to Florida to help me clean out the house and keep the garden in good shape until we sold the house. We decided that I would purchase an apartment at Glacier Hills Retirement Community, a beautiful complex just around the corner from the home of my cousins, Julie and Charles Ellis, in Ann Arbor. After I moved to Michigan in August 2005, I stayed with Julie and Charles for three weeks until my apartment was ready for me to move in. At Glacier Hills, I have a lovely apartment, and have met wonderful people. Meals are provided, and they have many cultural and social activities. I joined Temple Beth Emeth here in Ann Arbor, where my daughter Ruth, and cousin Julie, are also members.

It's unimaginable, all the things that are happening at Glacier Hills. We have concerts. We have lectures. We are very well informed. We have people who travel, because they're retired faculty members, and they show us not just maps, but we had a gentleman who showed us all of Afghanistan from years back, up to today, too. I try to participate in whatever I can.

Witness to History

Memories

When I came to the United States, I didn't talk about the camps to anyone. For years, talking about what happened to my family was hard. My uncles who had come to the U.S. before the war and I never talked about it. Nobody talked about it, not even with friends or other survivors. We wanted to forget it and start a new life. If you didn't want to talk about it, other people didn't want to hear about it either.

Later in Florida, a boy once asked me if I had dreams about the bad things. I told him,

> "All the time. You know what I dream about, I come to a big lake, and I can't cross it, no way to escape. I dream about the ghetto. It's like little holes in rocks that people are in – fixing shoes and fixing clothing. And I go there, and I can't find my way out. I come to a road, and there is no exit – there is always a barrier. Or somebody tells me that my parents are there. I can

Life&Times

Orlando Sentinel
OrlandoSentinel.com
SUNDAY, OCTOBER 24, 2004
SECTION F

MOVIES	POP CULTURE	BOOKS	INDEX
COMIC TEAM Director David O. Russell and actor Mark Wahlberg have plenty of heart. Page F3	**LITERARY LADY** In today's world, Jane Austen is our new Shakespeare. Page F9	**THE LEADING EDGE** Explore the link between moods, courage and creativity in *Exuberance*. Page F10	Gallery F2 Visual Arts F4 Best Sellers F11 Dear Abby F14

WITNESSES
TO THE DARKEST HOURS

By ALINE MENDELSOHN ● Sentinel staff writer

O ne woman escaped. One didn't see her parents for seven years. Another never saw her parents again. The stories are varied. But all of these women have one thing in common: They survived. Today, the Holocaust Memorial Resource and Education Center of Central Florida will unveil "Our Story: Experiences of Central Florida Women in the Holocaust," featuring photos and accounts from local survivors. Here are their stories.

SE The Orlando Sentinel, Tuesday, April 29, 1997   C-4A

Auschwitz survivor tells her story

☐ Longwood resident Lola Taubman shared her memories with the West Volusia Holocaust Memorial Council, composed of both Christians and Jews.

By Grover Austin
SENTINEL CORRESPONDENT

DELAND — Lola Taubman will never forget the night she saw her parents for the last time.

She had spent three agonizing days standing with them and the rest of her family inside a crowded boxcar. There was no food on board, no water, no toilets.

One woman gave birth; another went berserk. No one knew the destination or who would meet them when they arrived.

One cold April night 53 years ago, the train pulled into a place called Auschwitz, and a man named Joseph Mengele sent the elder Taubmans to their deaths with a wave of his hand. Their daughter, then 16 years old, lived to tell the story.

Taubman, 69, of Longwood recently was a guest speaker for the West Volusia Holocaust Memorial Council at Temple Israel in DeLand. The council was formed to bring the story of the Holocaust to local schools and to sponsor monthly events such as Taubman's speech.

"Out of all the Holocaust Councils across the country, this one is unusual in that it is made up of both Christians and Jews," said Marge Chase, who is in charge of the council. "We have a common purpose to see that what happened to Lola Taubman should not happen again."

Taubman was born and grew up in the small Czechoslovakian village of Svalava. What started out as a happy childhood ended abruptly when Adolf Hitler's troops invaded in 1938.

By 1942, the Nazi regime had become brutal, and in 1944 Jews from the area were placed on the train that would take them to one of the war's most horrible death camps.

Taubman will never forget seeing the man

SENTINEL FILE PHOTO
Sad past. Lola Taubman of Longwood was 16 when her parents died at Auschwitz.

who would tear her family asunder.

"He was a puffy-faced, arrogant and mean man," Taubman recalled of Mengele. "He had on an officer's uniform. Other officers had sticks and would push people to the right or to the left."

Other memories remain vivid, too, including the smoke-filled skies.

"We asked, 'What are those flames?' They said, 'It's a bakery.'"

Because Taubman was young and strong, she was spared the same fate as her parents. A harder fate awaited her, and the others separated with her, though, was a different kind of horror.

"The cruelty in which they welcomed us is indescribable," Taubman said. "They stripped us naked, shaved our heads and took a disinfectant from a bucket. We went into the sauna and showers. Officers came in with whips and

dogs and guns and walked among us."

By the next day, Taubman realized what had happened to her parents.

"We knew anybody sent on that side, you never heard from them again," Taubman said. "They were gassed. We saw these groups going into the crematorium, and they never came out. It was a nightmare."

To make the death of her parents even more unbearable, Taubman later found out that the night she arrived at Auschwitz there was a shortage of gas.

"They only partially gassed the people," she said. "The ovens couldn't handle so many corpses, so they would load them on a truck half dead, and they dumped my parents across the street from us and burned them alive."

During her imprisonment at Auschwitz, Taubman worked in the area between the barracks and the crematorium. It was her task to sort through what was left of her fellow prisoners' belongings.

One of the women with whom she was working found a coat that looked familiar. It had belonged to Taubman's father.

Inside one of its pockets was a picture of him that Taubman was able to keep close to her until the end of the war.

Taubman was at Auschwitz from April 1944 to January 1945. She then was transported to three other camps where her battle against persecution, hunger and sickness continued.

Finally, in April 1945, the group with which Taubman was marching met up with the Americans and Russians. Her journey to freedom could begin.

Taubman's story is one that will never be forgotten. Like so many Holocaust survivors, Taubman will be able to pass along her experiences to future generations.

She recently recorded her story on videotape for Steven Spielberg's Shoah project, a historical collection of survivors' stories to be used for education.

"They are the stories of how the Holocaust still affects the lives of people like Taubman. "You know what hurts the most?" Taubman said. "When holidays come. My children never had any grandparents."

Figure 25

Details from front page article,
April 29, 1997, the Orlando Sentinel Life and Times.

never see their faces. I wish I would dream about them more, and I could see them."

I have nightmares regardless whether I see a movie or not. I came to some function in the family in Great Neck, and we slept at my uncle's house. I was already married, and I woke up in the middle of the night saying, "My bed is on fire, my bed is on fire." I woke everybody up. I felt so bad disturbing everybody. In Florida, I dreamt that there were electrical wires under the bed and I jumped up and jumped over Sam and he almost got killed falling off the bed. I have nightmares to this day. It's not very pleasant. I see my husband, and we are going on a train and I cannot get close to him. I cannot touch him.

[*Lola's daughter, Ruth Taubman, remembers:*]

"Before my dad died, when we were growing up, particularly when we were teenagers, my mother woke up screaming at the top of her lungs maybe four to five nights a week – four out of seven nights a week."

Pictures take me back. One schoolgirl asked, "Is there anything that you have now that you had before?" And I said,

"I am so glad that you asked this question, because I forget to mention it. After the war, I didn't go home to my hometown, but my cousins did. After they emptied the Jewish homes, everybody took what they could or they wanted, they took the garbage that was left to the city dump. When my cousins were liberated after that war, they went there, and they found my parents' picture. So I have a small snapshot that was taken in 1936. And somebody else gave me a little picture – a group picture and I was in it. So I have just a few pictures. And I had them enlarged, and I made copies and I gave them to my children."

Now I think it's important to talk about it, because you never know when it can happen again. There are too many anti-Semites. You know, on one occasion, while speaking at a school in Orlando, a boy who was a Russian immigrant told me his father had told

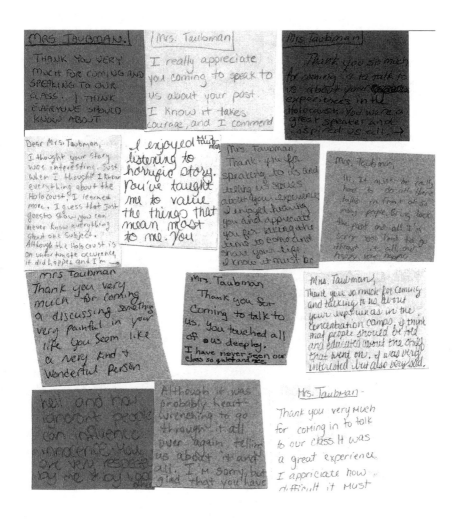

Figure 26

Selection from a pile of thank you notes on scraps of colored
construction paper, sent by students to Lola Taubman after
she spoke in their classroom. Undated, but representative of the
response to her sharing of her story.

him the Holocaust never happened. I was surprised to hear that Ann Arbor was established by Germans. Many people here are of German descent. They are kind to me, but I wonder what they think. They feel sorry for me that I went through that.

Telling the Story

In Florida, I was active with other survivors. A small office run by Tess Wise was the beginning of the Holocaust Center in Orlando. She is a very smart and able person who is very bright, smart and knew languages, and she started it. Her husband is a developer in Florida. They paid for the building in Maitland, outside of Orlando. Little by little people gave them money. We joined fund-raising dinners. I was very involved with the Holocaust Center. I became very involved in the Teachers' Institute, held every summer. I spoke to the teachers about my experiences in the Holocaust. On one occasion, one of the teachers ran out to get her tape recorder in order to record my story. The teacher sent me the tape.

I was interviewed for the Holocaust Center of Central Florida, and they have a copy of the tape.[10] I was also interviewed for Steven Spielberg's Shoah Project, by a woman, was trained to do these interviews, and who came from Boca Raton to our home in Longwood. I don't know if they gave a copy of it to the [United States] Holocaust Museum in Washington. I spoke at Rollins College in Winter Park and outlying areas far away. They were very nice. I spoke in another town on the way to Daytona Beach. And I also spoke at many schools in the Orlando area.

---

10   In her notes about the interviews she had with Lola, Velma Grasseler noted that Lola was interviewed for the collection of survivors' interviews at the Holocaust Museum in Maitland, Florida. A portion of her talk was also being shown continuously with excerpts from other survivors' interviews in the exhibition room of the Holocaust Center of Central Florida.

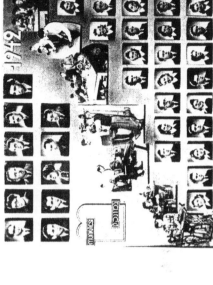

TO THE TEACHERS WHO INSPIRED US
TO LOVE ISRAEL,
TO THE STUDENTS WHO SHARED
THESE FEELINGS WITH US,
TO ALL WHO SUPPORTED
AND HELPED TO MAINTAIN
THIS WONDERFUL INSTITUTION,
THE ONE AND ONLY
HEBREW GYMNASIUM
IN MUNKACS

"TODA RABA"
THE ORGANISING COMMITTEE

Figure 27

Selected pages
from
Program
for Florida
reunion,
June 17-19,
1992,
of survivors
who
were students
at the
Munkacs
Hebrew
Gymnasium.

[*Ruth Taubman adds:*] [11]

"Even though it's privately funded, the state sent teachers and educators from all over Florida to be taught how to teach Holocaust education because it was required by their curriculum in the state in the later eighties and early nineties."

In Ann Arbor I have continued to speak about my experience at Temple Beth Emeth, and in schools. I spoke to my grandson Henry's middle school class at Forsythe Middle School. The students sat in a semi-circle around me and were so attentive you could hear a pin drop. I have found that telling my story in school is so important, because there is still so much ignorance in the world.

[*The Holocaust Memorial Resource and Education Center of Florida, in their Winter 2006 publication recognized Lola's power as a speaker:*]

"One of the most effective ways to teach about the Holocaust is through survivor testimony. We have been extremely fortunate over the years to have several members of the community who have generously made themselves available to speak to schools and community groups about their experiences.

"Two of our most effective speakers have been Helen Greenspun and Lola Taubman. ... "Lola Taubman recently moved to Michigan to be close to her family, and will no longer be available to speak to central Florida groups on behalf of the center. Born in Czechoslovakia, she endured imprisonment at Auschwitz where her entire family was killed. As she spoke to schoolchildren and other groups, she brought a clearer understanding of the enormous human cost of Hitler's war. "

---

11   Lola and Ruth Taubman interview with Professor Sidney Bolkosky, December 22, 2009, online archive, UM-Dearborn Voice/Vision Holocaust Survivor Oral History Archive.

Connecting with Survivors

A boy in a classroom in Florida asked me in 1995 if I kept in touch with my Uncle Louis who survived and was then in New York. My answer was:

> "Yes. We have Rosh Hashanah in the fall, which is the Jewish New Year. 50 cousins—2nd and 3rd generation—meet there every time. They dread to see the day when my uncle wouldn't be here any more, and we wouldn't have these gatherings. We try to keep in touch. I know about all my cousins. In Israel, on my mother's side, I have four cousins, and on my father's side, I have two cousins. And the rest of them are in New York, and in Michigan. We attend whatever festivity there is." [12]

A girl in the same class asked me how I found out the fate of people I met when I was in the concentration camps. I told her, "We talk. We survivors keep in touch. We call on the telephone. We hear from each other." I keep in touch with people in Miami and New York and Los Angeles. And we hear from each other what is happening. Ruben Strauss, the non-Jewish student in the Munkacs Hebrew Gymnasium, whose family rescued the principal's son (because a principal had let Ruben study at our school), had become an engineer in Hungary. He found out who was alive and he sent his picture—his class picture.

I keep in close contact with my family on my father's side. I try on my mother's side. There are not many left. We are very close with all the cousins. We know about every cousin. Some relatives were with me in the camps. There were ten of us. We didn't work together, but were in the same camp.

I have been to Israel several times to see survivors. I went after the 1967 war, in 1968—by myself because Sam had to work to do. I had the reunions of the Hebrew high school, with all the teachers.

---

12   Louis and Magda's older daughter, Susan Goldstein, carries on this Rosh Hashanah tradition to this day with a gathering of the New York-based members of the family. Their younger daughter, Julie Ellis, hosts a yearly Passover Seder for the Michigan-based family.

At the first one, several teachers survived and they came. They are all gone now. The Birnbaum sisters were there, the ones who were forced to sing for the officers in Auschwitz. After the war, two of them got married and went to Israel, and I met them there. I also met again their brother, who played the accordion at the reunion. He was so touched. He couldn't kiss the professors enough. It was beautiful.

The second reunion was very nice. Aunt Magda and Uncle Louis, we all went. It was amazing how many people from our school were there. One of my professors was in the same kibbutz where my cousins were. So that was very nice The Birnbaum brother was a teacher in a small kibbutz. He married a woman who lost her husband in the war. I went to his kibbutz with Magda and Louis. It was a kibbutz not far from the Sea of Galilee. We met about every three or four years. We met once in Los Angeles, once in Clearwater, Florida. Each year there is less and less of us left.

Return to Carpathian Mountains and Hungary[13]

In 1993, my husband Sam and I went on a visit to Czechoslovakia with my Uncle Louis and Aunt Magda and their two children, Julie and Susie. Sam did not come to the village with the cemetery but stayed in Budapest. He didn't know anything about that place.

[*Julie Ellis adds some details about Lola's trip to Budapest:*]

"We rushed onto Delta flight #144 to Budapest and begged the crew to delay our departure while we waited for Lola to meet up with us. She was delayed coming from Orlando. Unfortunately, the flight could wait no longer and we left

---

13   Lola's Uncle Louis and Aunt Magda Goldstein wrote a short record of this trip. Their daughter Julie Ellis wrote an independent and more detailed account of her experiences on this trip. Julie plans to write something in future that draws on both accounts. In this text, therefore, I include only small excerpts that complement Lola's narrative of her memories. [Louis, Magda, and Julie all use the Hungarian spelling "Szolyva" for the name of Lola's hometown. Throughout the rest of the book, we identify the town as "Svalava", the Czech spelling, which appears in Lola's documents and in photo inscriptions.]

hoping Lola would somehow connect to Budapest. She missed our flight by only a few minutes and was placed on a Singapore Airlines flight to Budapest via Frankfurt instead. .... We arrived at Budapest's Ferihegy Airport at 8:40 AM local time and took a cab to the Budapest Hilton Hotel .... Lola arrived around 5 PM, without luggage, but with a well-stocked carry-on bag. Luckily, she had enough clothes for our journey the next day to the Carpathian Mountains, and even had many of the gifts she had brought for the people there."

Munkacs

In Munkacs, We found a paper goods store which once supplied the school. The City Hall was still there, two stories high. Around the corner was the shop where my mother used to go to buy some material to have a coat made. Next to the City Hall there used to be a kosher restaurant, no longer operating by the time we came. We ordered salami and hot dogs. The only familiar things were the places that had once been little stores.

We found the Munkacs Hebrew Gymnasium. The building was still there. It was summertime, so there were no classes. We knocked, and a Russian woman came and said, "It's vacation. You can't come in." She didn't know who we were, and they didn't want any strangers in the school. I said, "I went to this school, and I want to see what it is like." Magda, too, went to the school. So, they let us in. We went to the second floor, and found that our principal's art was no longer on the hallway walls, and everything was more dirty. They had a teacher's conference going on. We introduced ourselves to those at the conference, and gave them some gifts. The people couldn't believe it, and said, "We will have some champagne for you."

[*Louis and Magda Goldstein shared their impressions of the visit to Magda's and his former schools:*]

"Naturally, we entered the Hebrew Gymnasium, where there were a few teachers gathering. When they found out

Figure 28

Magda and Louis
Goldstein, with
Lola Taubman,
standing in the
former Korzo street
in Svalava, where
Louis's candy store
once stood.
photo taken by
Susan Goldstein,
in 1993.

that Lola and Magda went to school there, they opened up a bottle of champagne in our honor. Afterwards, we saw the Hungarian Business School (Kereskedelmiy) [where Louis went to school]."

[*Julie Ellis adds interesting details about the school visit:*]

"[The Munkacs Hebrew Gymnasium] is now a technical trade school, similar to a junior college.... School was not in session, but we went inside and walked through the halls. Mom and Lola remembered eating their lunch and practicing their lessons there. We met a group of teachers who invited us into one of the classrooms. .... Before we left, we gave them gifts of calculators, pens, and cosmetics."

Svalava

In Svalava, the City Hall was still there. But when we came to where our house had been, there was a huge apartment house the Russians had built. The only other familiar things were some little houses, the building that once housed the apothecary, and some buildings that had once been little stores. One store once had buttons and bows. The building where Uncle Louis had his candy store was also still standing there.

[*Louis and Magda Goldstein on the visit to Svalava:*]

"Finally, we arrived to the main road of Szolyva[14]. The old village main street had disappeared. Everything in the area around the Catholic church had disappeared. They tore it down. The main road was widened and they built several story high buildings. .... Lola's family house had been torn down and replaced with a multi-story building. The old City Hall is across the street from where Lola's family's house had been. The Temple, across the street from Joseph Goldstein's house, became a bread factory."

---

14   Louis Goldstein and his daughter, Julie Ellis, both use the Hungarian spelling of Lola's birth city.

[Julie Ellis on the visit to Svalava:]

" [W]e telephoned Mr. Kirschenbaum, the last Jewish man living in Szolyva.... [who] keeps the key to the Jewish cemetery in Szolyva, and after we went to pick him up, he took us there.... Mom's parents and Lola's brother and grandparents were buried in this cemetery, but unfortunately we couldn't find their exact gravestones. We held hands, and said Kaddish, and cried.... [On the street near Magda's former house,] Lola remembered who had lived in all the houses.... We walked up the street into town and passed the doctor's offices and police station on the left. On the left corner at the main street stands the original City Hall. Across the main street from the City Hall had been Lola's family's house. It has been torn down and replaced by very modest apartment buildings and shops. Turning right from the City Hall onto the former Korzo, is the corner where the Bodek family's store had been. Further down and across the Korzo, is where Dad had his candy store."

Palos (Pavlovo) and Izvor

The Ukrainian man that took care of the cemetery [in Pavlovo (Palos)] sent a message that if we could get some paint, he could paint the lettering on the gravestones to restore them. So my Aunt Magda went to the Metropolitan Museum of Art in New York and got some good paint. We came to the village. The Ukrainian man lived in a one-room house that was his kitchen and his bedroom and everything. He was very pleased. We brought him shoes and sweaters and sardines.

[Julie Ellis on the visit to the cemetery:]

"We drove from Szolyva to Palos (Pavlovo). ... to a Jewish cemetery there. The cemetery is tended by an old man, Mr. Lizanec.... Birds were singing and bees buzzing. The cemetery is well kept up by Mr. Lizanec. There were some wildflowers growing, but the grass was mowed. We found the graves of Dad's parents, Zev and Esther Goldstein, which are not next to each other.... Everything ... is written in Hebrew.... We said Kaddish and tried to soak in the beauty of this wonderful place."

When we arrived to grandmother's village, Izvor, it is still a small village. It was dusty. The Russians built a new bridge and they took away the railroad. There is no bus, and people came to see the big car we were in. Only half of Grandmother's house survived. After the war, originally Uncle Martin came back from Russia, and he lived in Grandma's house. The villagers said to Uncle Louis, "Who are you?" They wanted to know who he was and he told them his name and they said, "You were my teacher." They also asked what happened to Esther-ka, the Ukrainian version of my grandmother Esther's name. They forgot that luckily she died of natural causes, while my mother and father were in Slovakia.

[Louis and Magda Goldstein on the visit to Izvor:]

"We found Louis' house, but only half of it remains. But, it is still there. Nobody lives there. The river still flows behind the house. Across the street from the house was a hazelnut tree. Every child looked at that hazel nut tree when we were young. The small gauge railroad track that was across from the house does not exist anymore."

Coda

Reflections

I didn't apply for reparations for a long time. I never got one penny. When the registration started for that, I didn't believe it would happen, and I didn't register. Later on, I wanted to register, and they said it was too late. I was entitled to the money, but the Russian Jews working in the claims office wanted to see my tax forms, and they said, "You are earning too much money from Social Security." They wanted to know how much money my husband made. They did find a little insurance that my father had.

Figure 29

Lola
Taubman
speaking
at
Glacier Hills
Retirement
Community,
Ann Arbor,
Michigan,
June 10,
2011.
Photo by
Diane
Kirkpatrick.

I am very happy to be living in Michigan near my children, Ruth and Richard, and my cousin Julie Ellis, and their families. They have all been so helpful to me and have been wonderful. I couldn't have made this move without my wonderful family.

My daughter Ruth and Bill's sons Henry and Jack are both athletic and smart and loving. We celebrated both of their Bar Mitzvahs, after Sam passed away. In California, Alyssa and Robert's daughters, Talia and Mia are talented in both music and art. I traveled to California where they live for Talia's and Mia's Bat Mitzvahs. In August 2009, my son Richard, who had been divorced for several years, married Alison Lemeshow, who is a lovely, smart, and kind woman. I am so happy that Richard is settled and happy. Richard's daughters, Rachel and Danielle, are both lovely young women who have been helpful and loving. I love all my grandchildren, especially the "necky" kisses that I give and get when I see them.

My cousin Susan Goldstein (Uncle Louis and Aunt Magda's daughter) continues to be one of my closest cousins. I babysat with Susie while her sister Julie was born. Susie continues the legacy of her parents by keeping our family together. There is something special about Susie and her sister Julie that's indescribable. They inherited their parents' good hearts, always giving to others all they can. I love giving "necky" kisses to my cousin Jonathan, Julie and Charlie Ellis's son. I am also happy to be close to Al Taubman and his family. Al includes me in all the Taubman family events.

We are considered a special family that keeps in touch with each other. I keep in touch with all my cousins, especially those who survived the war: Sandor, Irene, Manyi, Manya, Hersi, and their families. All the cousins gather for holidays and special occasions: the Goldsteins, the Taubmans, and the Oberländers. I'm lucky to have survived after losing my whole family in the Holocaust, and to be embraced by our greater family throughout these years.

Final Thoughts

Through everything, I never resented being Jewish. I was born that way, and that's what I'm going to be. I never considered turning Catholic or anything else. And I don't hide my Jewishness either. You know what hurts most? That when holidays come, or when my children were born, my children never had any grandparents. If I was sick, I didn't have my mother's warm hand to hold me.

Acknowledgements

I would not be here without my devoted daughter, Ruth, who has been with me through good and bad, every moment of her life; her love for me is indescribable. I greatly cherish the constant care and love from my son, Richard, who is always so good to me. I also deeply appreciate all of the love and efforts of my daughter, Alyssa, especially when I really need her.

I want to express my love for my outstanding aunt and uncle, Magda and Louis, my constant protection and helpers throughout my life; during the war, and in Prague, Brooklyn, and Detroit. Their daughters, Julie and Susie, continue to be my closest cousins, and follow their parents' role in my life.

I would like to acknowledge the first person to produce my recollections in written form, Velma Grasseler, a volunteer at The Holocaust Memorial Resource and Education Center of Central Florida. I also greatly appreciate Sid Bolkolsky, Director of the University of Michigan Dearborn's Voice/Vision Holocaust Survivor Oral History Archive, whose interview with me made my story available online. My entire family and I are extremely grateful to Diane Kirkpatrick, without whose endless hours of hard work, dedication, tremendous patience, and friendship, this book would not be possible.

Finally, to Sam, my beloved husband of 51 years, who was so devoted to me. I miss him, and dream about him every night.

Made in the USA
San Bernardino, CA
31 January 2016